Expecting Excellence

Expecting Excellence

Creating Order Out of Chaos in a School District

Judith A. Shipengrover
James A. Conway

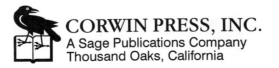

CORWIN PRESS, INC.
A Sage Publications Company
Thousand Oaks, California

For information address:

Corwin Press, Inc.
A Sage Publications Company
2455 Teller Road
Thousand Oaks, California 91320
E-mail: order@corwin.sagepub.com

SAGE Publications Ltd.
6 Bonhill Street
London EC2A 4PU
United Kingdom

SAGE Publications India Pvt. Ltd.
M-32 Market
Greater Kailash I
New Delhi 110 048 India

Printed in the United States of America

Library of Congress Cataloging-in-Publication Data

Shipengrover, Judith A.
    Expecting excellence: Creating order out of chaos in a school
district / Judith A. Shipengrover, James A. Conway.
       p.   cm.
    Includes bibliographical references (p.   ).
    ISBN 0-8039-6285-1 (cloth : acid-free paper). — ISBN 0-8039-6286-X
(pbk. : acid-free paper)
    1. School improvement programs—New York (State)—Case studies.
    2. School districts—New York (State)—Administration—Case studies.
I. Conway, James A.   II. Title.
LB2822.83.N7S55   1996
371.2'009747'97—dc20   96-10088

This book is printed on acid-free paper.

96 97 98 99 10 9 8 7 6 5 4 3 2 1

Production Editor:	Vicki Baker
Typesetter/Designer:	Christina Hill
Cover Designer:	Marcia Finlayson

Contents

Preface

Dissatisfaction, criticism, and reform initiatives are not new to American education. The most recent efforts to transform K-12 education began in the early 1980s. Since then, educators have been bombarded with recommendations for change, sometimes with remarkable results. For example, imagine schools where

- decisions are not just a series of political compromises;
- instruction is diverse enough to ensure that all students are engaged in learning;
- teachers, parents, administrators, custodians, and bus drivers together engage in research as a process to solve problems; and
- teachers and staff determine the content of staff development.

These are just some of the positive images of transformed schools. But creating new structures is not simply a task of dreaming.

In the wake of the reform efforts of the 1980s, researchers looked intensely at effective schools to identify elements that set them apart. The literature is replete with descriptions of characteristics that lead to excellence (e.g., Firestone & Corbett, 1988). Yet, as Kowalski and Reitzug (1993) suggest, we still know far too little about how such

> values and beliefs support effective performance and become a part of the school's normative structure. For instance, how do risk-taking teachers and principals affect student performance? Does risk taking become the expected behavior in a

school through formal decisions, or does it occur through an evolutionary process? (p. 315)

Stemming from the notion that schools and the roles of educators must change, a second stream of research looked for answers to such questions as, What changed? Who led the change? How much time did it take? These, too, remain monumental questions for school administrators. Although the need for reform is evident, however, many doubt that the task can be accomplished and critics have concluded that school reform during the 1980s was a story of failure (Cetron & Gayle, 1991). For this reason, a clear picture of how one school district's transformation, begun in the 1980s, was sustained and did not revert to traditional practices is an important story to tell. It can be useful in providing lessons for success and adding insights to the questions that have eluded researchers.

This book is about the Kenmore-Town of Tonawanda (Ken-Ton) Union Free School District, outside Buffalo, New York. Beginning in 1981, Ken-Ton, even then a respected and well-recognized district, successfully transformed itself from a complacent, bureaucratic, closed organization with less than challenging expectations of students and staff to one where excellence is expected, power is widely shared, and teaching and learning come first. The transformation, which began long before externally imposed mandates were written into policy, resulted in a culture of quality and continuous improvement.

Two features make this book unique. First, although many books describe successful reforms, few accounts are told directly from the perspectives of those who lived through the change as they progressed through each transition. Second, few books provide the details of how things critical to success were set in motion—such things as

- how the district's readiness for change was determined;
- how structures were created for guiding the change;
- how principals and administrators were prepared for the change;
- how the district proceeded toward team structures and redesigned processes and systems to be congruent with a decentralized environment;
- how people and teams adjusted to team dynamics and the pitfalls they experienced; and
- how to jump-start teams while they are in progress.

Who Should Read This Book

The intended audience is students and practitioners of education administration who find they need to take a fresh look at their beliefs about schools and how to improve them. As external mandates authored by legislators have intensified, our worst fears are that the pursuit of excellence may have become just another fad in education. That is, we fear that the subject of excellence (which is at the core of what reform is all about) has lost its significance among practicing educators.

School administrators played a central role in transforming the Ken-Ton schools but they were not heroes or magicians. For them, the change was both a threat and an opportunity. The traditional frameworks they experienced as students, and continued to experience as practitioners, no longer provided substantial security. Transformation was a threat to safe and familiar beliefs, values, and practices that gave meaning to their jobs. They had to learn to facilitate and coach rather than to lead with a club; to align individual, team, school, and district goals; and to build an organization that is continuously learning and improving.

Some of the things that happened along the way were expected; others were a surprise. Some they were prepared for; others they were not. Nevertheless, they are leaders who brought together teachers, parents, students, and others to create organizational structures that will meet instructional needs that extend into the 21st century.

The Main Themes of the Book

The title of this book introduces two paradoxical and contradictory themes. One theme is that of *chaos*. We use the word in the sense that Gleick (1987) proposes—to describe a system that is unstable. Others have called the same phenomenon a *mess*—that is, a system of problems or instabilities (Ackoff, 1974)—which is what Ken-Ton confronted at the beginning of its journey. We also use the term to capture the pace, complexity, novelty, risks, and nonstop challenges posed by the changes required to undertake such a journey.

The current turbulent environment of education requires a response so different from the traditional approach of diagnose-plan-implement-evaluate that only the term chaos expresses the dynamism, fluidity, and extraordinary complexity that contemporary education administrators face. Our hope is to help students, administrators, and teachers feel more friendly to chaos and to messes, for in the world of chaos, nothing ever works quite as it is intended or expected to.

A second theme of this book is that of order. In Part I, we present the evolution of the Ken-Ton district's improvement initiative. The chapters are full of the accounts of many of the individuals who participated in the 13-year journey (1981 to 1994). Part I is more a montage than it is a single, linear argument—a set of personalized accounts that lend themselves to a variety of literary methods. We have tried to be mindful of order and logic in the flow of our presentation of the chronology, but we realize that the overall organization may be elusive.

In Part II, we use familiar frameworks to interpret what is described in Part I. Without a set of alternative glasses through which to view the montage of Part I, we would compound the likelihood of supporting change as a trial-and-error process alone and a belief that crisis management is normal. Although we acknowledge that chaos is what systems deal with daily, we also believe that there are ways to cope with chaos so that change can be transferred to other times and places. The chapters of Part II provide frameworks that may explain what happened, help to predict when and how it might occur again, and provide practitioners with templates that make sense out of their own experiences.

Let the journey begin!

Acknowledgments

Many people played key roles in making this book possible. John Helfrich, retired superintendent of the Kenmore-Town of Tonawanda (Ken-Ton) Union Free School District, actively contributed challenging ideas and willingly shared insights. Grateful appreciation especially goes to Robert Freeland, retired deputy superintendent, whose patient support, exacting criticism, and insightful review made the book better than it possibly could have been otherwise. Most important, we acknowledge the contributions of more than 40 members of the Ken-Ton school community, past and present, whose words and recollections breathed warmth and life into this work. We thank them anonymously and hope we have done justice to their stories. We also wish to acknowledge Henry Mintzberg and | I | D | E | A | for the permission to reproduce or adapt their figures. Finally, each of us has special words of acknowledgment for our respective families.

From Judy: To my husband Bill, a master teacher, whose support and patience made the work not only possible but manageable; and to my daughter, Joanna, a vibrant example of the evolving nature of quality, my love and admiration.

From Jim: To acknowledge the support of my wife Linda, as a dedicated teacher and mother, but most of all as my best friend.

About the Authors

Judith A. Shipengrover is a curriculum consultant to the Robert Wood Johnson Generalist Initiative Project at the University of Buffalo School of Medicine, where she facilitates curriculum reform linked to the preparation of primary care physicians. She formerly was cofounder of the Management Training unit of the Center for Human Services at Buffalo State College, where she led a statewide study to identify competencies required for managing in health and human services agencies and managed the development of all training programs for managers of public agencies. She is the author of numerous training manuals and monographs. She received a B.S. from Kent State University in foreign language education, an M.A. from Teachers College, Columbia University, in student personnel administration, and a Ph.D. from the University of Buffalo in education administration.

James A. Conway is a professor at the University of Buffalo's Graduate School of Education. He has published in many journals and several books. During the past 35 years, he has been in higher education teaching research and educational administration at Buffalo State College, the University of Miami (Coral Gables), Didsbury College (England), University College Galway (Ireland), and the University at Buffalo, where he was chair of the Department of Educational Administration for 9 years. He holds a B.A. from the University at Albany, NY, an M.A. in educational administration from Teachers College, Columbia University, and the first doctorate (an Ed.D.) ever awarded by the University at Albany (1963).

Part I

The Ken-Ton School District and Its Chronology of Change

The descriptive aspect of educational criticism is essentially an "attempt to identify and characterize, portray or render in language the relevant qualities of educational life" (Eisner, 1994, p. 226).

The chapters in this first section of the book describe in detail the evolutionary process that occurred in the Kenmore-Town of Tonawanda (Ken-Ton) School District from the time of the change of superintendents in 1981 to the year in which that leader retired (1994) and a new superintendent was appointed. The focus is a dynamic and detailed description of the changes planned, the processes used, the behaviors observed, and the outcomes that materialized in the district. Our data for the descriptions come primarily from Shipengrover's (1994) dissertation, which focuses on understanding the quality improvement process in K-12 education by analyzing how the successful implementation of formal school improvement practices compares with the components considered to compose a total quality management system.

Via direct observations, document analysis, and interviews of administrators, teachers, support staff, board of education members, and external consultants, Shipengrover (1994) was able to capture the insights and perceptions of principal players in the Ken-Ton school improvement program (SIP). The interviews began with two broad questions:

- How did the school improvement process proceed?
- As you look back, can you see stages in its evolution?

Unlike the limiting nature of a closed questionnaire, the interview process gave participants an opportunity to raise questions and to share insights that Shipengrover (1994) had not anticipated. For this book, the dissertation data are supplemented by additional formal and informal interviews, as well as by long-term personal contacts both authors have had with the district personnel through university classes, surveys, and personal experiences such as serving on district planning and design teams.

Our purpose for Part I is to provide sufficient details for the reader to gain an understanding of how this district confronted the chaos of the 1980s to weave its way through 13 years to become recognized as an award-winning district. All too often, the chronicles of outstanding businesses, corporations, and schools focus almost exclusively on the leader. Our intent is to broaden the scope of analysis beyond such a singular focus so as to uncover other dimensions that may be even more important to the transformation process. What were the major structures and contextual elements of the process? What gave rise to it? What forms did it take and what sustained it over time? Such questions provide the backdrop for this inquiry.

Chapter 1 puts the district into context. Here we provide an overview of the environment, examining the community and the situation immediately prior to the appointment of the superintendent who was in office during the 13 years of the study. Chapter 1 also describes participants' perceptions of the first steps leading to the implementation of the SIP.

Chapter 2 describes the conceptual framework of the model of school improvement adopted by the district. It then shifts the emphasis temporarily to examine major strategies of change in the literature and how they relate to the stages this school district went through. The review is brief because there are as many conceptions of change and the change process as there are educators, or so it seems. The concept of stages is used as a template that, when applied to the Ken-Ton experience, provides a framework for organizing how participants understood and interpreted the historical processes and events through which the SIP evolved.

Chapter 3 describes how the district developed its guiding conceptualization, a stage that we identify as lasting 4 years—from 1982 to 1986. Some of the factors that helped initiate the pathway to school improvement included consistent attention to building trust between staff and senior administration and adopting practices that would increase the capacity of individual schools to make decisions about their own visions and goals. Such practices involved the use of team structures that required heavy investment in ongoing staff development focused on team visioning and consensus decision making.

Chapter 4 describes a stage that lasted approximately 4 years, from 1986 to 1990. During this stage, the skepticism with which staff had responded to the newness of the tasks and challenges of the first stage gave way to more than a grudging acceptance.

Chapter 5 presents the third stage of the school improvement initiative, which lasted from 1990 through 1992. This stage is characterized as one in which the SIP philosophy became accepted as standard practice in the district. At this point, after 8 years of implementation, almost all the school participants were reasonably aware of instances where shared decision making was used as standard practice.

By the end of the third stage of the SIP, after an 11-year focus on school improvement, Ken-Ton applied for and won the New York State Excelsior Award, an award based on the philosophy of total quality management (TQM). Chapter 6 describes the results of the self-assessment process that required the district to examine and document what it had been doing, only using a different set of criteria—the criteria of TQM. This chapter concludes with an identification of the key elements in the 11-year movement as abstracted from the words of the district personnel.

1

❧

In the Beginning

The District and the Community

Mentor You've begun your journey. At the start, confusion is to be expected.

Steve But I feel lost.

Mentor You want everything planned in advance. That's fine for a trip to Chicago. It won't work for a journey of the spirit. First, you have to get started. Move into uncharted territory. (adapted from Bolman & Deal, 1995, p. 46)

The story of the Kenmore-Town of Tonawanda (Ken-Ton) Union Free School District is a case study of a single school district. But why this district? Why do we choose this one as the focus of our study? There are several reasons; in brief, this district is typical of thousands of American school districts, and yet it is atypical for the unusual recognition it has received. To understand these reasons, we need to put the district in perspective.

First, the district typifies many of America's problem areas. It serves a large first-ring metropolitan suburb located between Buffalo and Niagara Falls, New York. The village of Kenmore, located within the town of Tonawanda, is one of the largest incorporated villages in the state. The two communities have a population of more than 80,000 and are in a relatively heavy industrial area. More than 95% of Ken-Ton's residents are Caucasian and 75% no longer have school-age children. The community, however, is often a first stop for families eager to leave the central city. The school district, therefore, has a diverse population of students in terms of income, culture, and national heritage. Family income ranges from substandard poverty level to high income, and the percentage of student turnover is high. For example, in one elementary school surrounded by middle-class housing, the children are from low-income families living in governmental housing projects and trailer parks, with 70% eligible for Chapter 1 funding; 81% live in single parent homes.

Second, the district moved through some distinct periods of growth and trauma prior to the period of our study. In 1955, there were fewer than five school buildings. Then the district experienced a period of rapid growth, reaching an apex in 1967. That year was also the beginning of a precipitous decline in population and student enrollments. During the next 20 years, the school population went from 22,000 to just over 8,000; with that decline, the district closed 16 of its 28 schools.

Third, the district experienced a revival marked by national recognition for the period of 1981 to 1995. A new superintendent was hired in 1981. From the very beginning, he challenged the entire district to become involved in a comprehensive school improvement program (SIP), applying a model designed for improving individual schools to improving an entire school district. Remember, this was 15 years ago, a time when many districts set up small projects with one or two schools, moved them outside the existing system, and operated them as distinct entities. Ken-Ton, on the other hand, went districtwide. Said a senior district administrator, "When you do that, you're going to get some turbulence, and the first few years were certainly turbulent!"

It is the unfolding and implementation of that process, its uncertain journey from turbulence to the time of its award-winning excellence in 1992, that is the period of intense study we present and analyze in this book. At the culmination of the period under study, student outcomes showed the following results (Keasling, 1992):

- Elementary reading, math, and writing scores moved upward, with more than 95% of the scores significantly above the state reference point.
- Mean verbal and math Scholastic Aptitude Test (SAT) scores increased steadily from 1987 on and consistently exceeded state and national means.
- The percentage of Ken-Ton seniors receiving scholarships increased from 15% to 23%.

- The percentage of seniors going on to higher education increased steadily from 75% to more than 85%; the drop-out rate declined from 4.6% to less than 1.5%.

In addition to student progress, there is evidence of increased community satisfaction. Since 1987, budgets and bond issues have been passed by considerable majorities, most with nearly 80% voting in favor. During the same period, incumbent board members were consistently reelected, despite an operating expense that grew from $40 million to over $80 million dollars annually. Furthermore, enrollment in the district's continuing education programs increased 81%.

Fourth, the district's 13-year improvement process resulted in 12 of the district's 13 schools receiving School of Excellence awards from New York state. Three of those received the award twice. Seven schools have been recognized as National Schools of Excellence. In 1992, the district as a whole won the prestigious New York State Governor's Excelsior Award for Quality in the Education Sector, an award based on the principles and practices of total quality management. This was the first time any school district in the nation had won a Malcolm Baldrige-type award. As an Excelsior winner, Ken-Ton is a model or benchmark district, recognized by external quality experts as demonstrating superior quality practices. The advantage of targeting Ken-Ton as the subject of our study is that the criteria for the award were developed through the consensus of independent experts.

Finally, there is a strong sense of pride and ownership in the schools. Members of the school community truly believe their school or district is better than the next. And they are the first to tell people why. Their excitement and enthusiasm are contagious. They deserve to tell their own story, and to tell it in their own words.

The Conditions Leading to Change: The Historical Context

To understand more fully the success of the SIP, one must understand its evolution in a historical context. Ken-Ton participants prefaced their discussions with us by providing historical information about life in the district in its early years. They described the forces leading to the need for improvement and the early first steps in initiating the improvement process.

The Period of Prelude to Change

The period prior to the 1970s was described as one of demographic growth as well as cultural stability for the district. From 1956 to 1968, the number of the buildings in the district grew from 5 to 28 to accommodate an enrollment that peaked in 1968 at nearly 23,000 students.

Growth and Stability

Almost paradoxically, district members describe this period of building and population growth as one of stability, as there was minimal turnover in the board of education, community pride in the schools was level, and administrators were typically traditional in leadership style. A union leader, for example, points out that, "since 1910 only a limited number . . . served on the board of education . . . the commitment of people has been long term, and although there were critics, rarely was there a community group organized enough to defeat budgets or candidates." A consultant to the district feels that a five-member board was a stabilizing factor: "When board size is larger—seven or nine members is common in many districts—there is more potential for factions."

A parent's unwavering enthusiasm about the district captures the community's pride in the schools: "I've always thought this was a wonderful district. I went to school here from kindergarten all the way through. When I moved out of state people would say, 'Wow, you come from such a great district!' "

Stable leadership was apparent in two ways. In one context, peaceful labor relations seemed to be linked to a union leadership that was stable and that, early on, operated by consensus. A union member points out that, "we've had the same president for 20 years and the same nucleus of executive board members for 15 years. It has always operated by consensus."

A second aspect of leadership concerned the styles of the district's administrators during this period, which participants describe as paternalistic and top down. According to one observer: "There was a

15-year-old 'good old boy' network which permeated the district and was difficult to influence." Another observer confirms this perception, saying it was difficult for administrators to share power, and as a result they "didn't pay attention to people who had good ideas." Underlying this change-resistant perspective was the tendency to blame staff rather than to offer assistance or resources for problem solving. According to one administrator, "If you had a problem, former superintendents would . . . blame you, saying, 'What the hell are you going to do about it?' And 'You better do something about it now!' "

But the recollections are not all negative. At least one administrator (a superintendent) is remembered as a statesman: "A scholar-administrator, he loved to discuss and debate issues. He was a father figure. He brought staff into the district. He nurtured them. He promoted them. He saw them as *his* staff."

Lack of Innovation and Risk Taking

A concomitant outcome of this culture was the tendency to avoid taking risks. Three outstanding factors were apparent. One was a "graying" faculty. The least tenured teacher in the district had been there 12 years. People were entrenched in the status quo, with a set of habits that included pride in the work of the past and living on prestige from established reputations. One teacher recalls the times this way:

> We all came pretty much in the early 1960s and we've all stayed. I think we had gotten to a point in our lives professionally that we were just kind of stagnant. There weren't any new teachers to give freshness or new ideas.

Further evidence comes from a board member, who observes that "trying and failing was something that had never been allowed to happen. You really had to be on your toes. People were afraid to speak up and suggest things because they didn't want to fail."

From a policy point of view, an administrator notes, "For so many years if you had an idea . . . you could implement it in your own program as long as it wasn't against the philosophy of the school. And if it was . . . the answer was 'No! Absolutely not!' " From a teacher's perspective, a lack of risk taking was exacerbated by little staff recognition: "For so long in this district some really good teachers went unnoticed doing great things."

Finally, the district's hiring practices signaled that it wanted to maintain a closed system. There was little staff diversity and there was a long-standing norm to hire mainly from within the community. Recounting her own hiring experience, one teacher explains, "I didn't go to school in this district so, when I got my job here I was taken aback when somebody said, 'Well, how on earth did you get a job here?' The feeling often expressed was that Kenmore only hired their own."

An Unsettling Era of Unrest

In contrast to the 1960s, the 1970s were marked by trauma in the form of redistricting, changing staff relationships, the perception of declining standards, and an unsuccessful attempt at school reform. Enrollment was declining, the student population was changing as a result of the movement out of cities into the suburbs, and, with the advent of collective bargaining, teacher-administrator relationships were beginning to change.

Redistricting

By 1970, homes stood on every housing lot in the district, creating neighborhoods with small neat houses tightly lining the streets. As the availability of homes for new families declined and the average age of residents increased, the student population decreased.

Redistricting became a reality beginning in 1974. It was obvious that the district could not support all its 28 buildings. From 1977 through 1980, there was a contentious period of downsizing and building closings, necessitated by the precipitous drop in the student population from nearly 23,000 (in 1968) to 15,000 (in 1977). Thirteen buildings were closed and 600 teachers, many with more than 17 years of experience, were excised through attrition or layoffs.

As a result of the closings, layoffs, and reassignments, the morale of both staff and community declined. It would be an understatement to say the people were upset. Large community contingents attended board meetings. When a student was reassigned to a different school, parents complained vociferously. After all, they were seeing treasured memories erased. Schools that were attended by three or four generations of the same family were now on the cutting block.

For many staff, the administrative style of a superintendent hired early in that era exacerbated the unrest. In their view, he was brought in as a "gun slinger" to oversee and complete the process of downsizing. Because he was from outside the system, he did not have the nurturing, fatherly relationship with staff that his predecessor had. They were not his people. Consequently, he was viewed as a "hardnosed hatchet man who was more concerned with making tough decisions about closing buildings than he was about learners, programs, teachers, and staff." On the other hand, some district personnel were sympathetic with his role:

> The man had to make some very tough decisions in terms of closing buildings. It had to be done. I don't know whether the previous superintendent wanted to make those tough decisions. He retired before most of them were made. I think people who were around in those days would now say, "While we didn't like what he had to do, it had to be done," and Kenmore is probably better for it because we couldn't have operated with all those schools.

State and National Trends

Underlying local morale issues were national and state trends that contributed to staff skepticism about impending reform. The late 1960s and early 1970s marked the beginning of the slippage of academic standards nationally, cited as a decline in SAT scores. Locally, there was the perception that Ken-Ton's standards were also being compromised. An administrator explains that

> coming out of the 1970s, where everybody was into self-esteem and wanting people to feel positive, there ended up a lowering of academic standards. Kids were getting through, graduation rates were good . . . but the standards and expectations were too low. Kids fully capable of Regents level work were in basic classes.

A related element was an increase in union influence and power. State laws gave unions the power of formal grievances, negotiation, and third-party arbitration. In Ken-Ton, as a result of the massive layoffs and reassignments, tenured teachers with 17 and 18 years of experience were laid off. Not surprisingly, these educators "took every avenue available to protect themselves." They raised concerns over summer school assignments as well as cutbacks and layoffs. As one teacher describes it, "the administration were on one side, and the teachers on the other. We seldom talked to each other."

In the late 1970s and early 1980s, Albert Shanker, president of the American Federation of Teachers, began talking at the national level about the need for improvement and self-reflection in education. The Ken-Ton union leaders, whom members perceived as not traditionally "on the soft side of educational issues," responded to this charge. They urged members to gamble on reform, recognizing its value in establishing a climate that in the long run would benefit more people. A central office administrator attributes that openness in part to a superintendent who, in the early 1970s, had set a tone for informal negotiations conducted through a labor relations specialist:

> The reason we've had the relationships we've had with the union had to do with the fact that the president was dealing with a labor relations person, not the superintendent or the board. The superintendent hired a private sector executive, who had also been active as a board member, to work in labor-management relations. The foresight of having someone from the outside, a noneducator, was just a critical thing. It laid the groundwork for contract settlements accomplished through layers of informal contacts and relationships. A climate of trust was established in the mid-1970s, nearly 10 years before we even began the SIP!

Early Reform Efforts

Yet another influence on the district's morale problems was a late 1970s state-level initiative to reform schools. Conceptually, the state's model, known as Project Redesign, advocated shared decision making or site-based management. Although the specifics of the program are only vaguely remembered by the staff, the program had a lasting, negative influence on their attitudes toward school improvement efforts for many years to come. Participants in the program describe it as

> a big project that lasted maybe 2 years and then was dropped. The superintendent set up committees to assess community needs and get parents involved. Some of us were drafted to go door to door surveying parents about how the schools could

be improved. People put in a lot of extra after-school hours and it didn't go anywhere. A report was written which identified district priorities, and then parceled them out to schools—top down. But it was all lip service! It sat in a file. Nobody looked at it.

Staff not yet employed by the district at that time recall the jaded attitudes the project evoked toward any school improvement efforts, including those yet to come:

I was not around when Project Redesign occurred, but a lot of people who were [later] asked to be on school planning teams came in with that on their minds. You would constantly hear them mention, "We're not going to participate in this because it's another Project Redesign. We'll put all this time in it and it's going to go away. We won't see any results."

Administrators validate that feeling and explain the power of the reactions:

Those involved did see it as something which had merit, and they did buy into it as a real significant change. You talked to constituent groups. You got input from them. You tried it out. These are all things that, at that time, we had not been doing. The frustration was there was no follow through, no structure, no expectation that anyone really do it. The reward for people who did it was more meetings! And they came up with pro-posals which they were supposed to accomplish with "smoke and mirrors" because there wasn't any money.

Against the backdrop of layoffs, declining staff morale, parental dissatisfaction, and an unsuccessful short-term attempt at school im-provement planning, the board of education acknowledged a need "to get back to the business of educating kids as a primary function." The board wanted leadership that would specify and define a direction for the district. An administrator captures the subtle nature of the shift: "The change was not about moving the district from bad to good, but from getting us out of a 'maintenance' or status quo mind set."

The Beginnings of the Change Story

In November 1981, the school board confirmed Jack Helfrich as its new superintendent. In sharp contrast to the shared decision-making practices for which the district would later become noted, only the board was involved in selecting and interviewing finalists, an approach consistent with the top-down style that characterized the district's leadership in the 1970s. One administrator recalls that "there was a great deal of secrecy around the appointment. We didn't meet the candidates when they were brought in and taken on tours . . . and if there was a job description, it was not the result of public input."

Although Helfrich brought with him a varied administrative background (elementary and high school principal, assistant superintendent, superintendent), what appealed to board members was his ability to perceive the issues in the district and his ability to provide a vision. The new superintendent likewise expresses enthusiasm for the possibilities Ken-Ton offered:

> I was a superintendent in a very small but wealthy district down-state and wanted a larger district. Ken-Ton was a large district in a depressed area. It looked like a whale of a challenge. School improvement is part of my psyche. I've done it wherever I've been—but never as intensively or as broad-based as here.

Helfrich perceived the enormity of the task and from the very start understood the critical importance of having adequate time. He asked the board to give him 2 or 3 years as a grace period to put a process in place that would facilitate the district's quest for quality and excellence.

Reorganization Begins

In the spring of 1982, Helfrich challenged the entire district to become involved in a comprehensive SIP. The program began with a reorganization of the central office, signaling the beginning of a shift in philosophy that Helfrich describes as "getting people who are decision makers by trade—the people who hand out decisions and money—to become facilitators and supporters and cheerleaders." The district was organized by functions (personnel, curriculum, finance).

Everyone was concerned about making sure his or her function was well run. But what they didn't have was responsibility for student learning. Helfrich was seeking a way to give people at the school level the freedom and flexibility they needed to do their jobs within a framework that included district perspectives and district accountability.

The deputy superintendent recalls the first diagram he saw of how staff were to be rearranged:

> You walk into his (Helfrich's) office and all over the wall he's got diagrams made with magic markers on the "white board." It symbolized a paradigm shift from the top-down approach to decision making to one of collaboration. No one had ever . . . talked things out before. In the past, you sat down in a meeting to be "told." Now, the whole discussion process was recorded, erased . . . things were clearly up for modification.

Relocation

One of Helfrich's first tasks was to flatten the organizational hierarchy, relocating central office staff using a logic that called for "putting people together who did similar things." He moved his own office next to the boardroom and put business and personnel staff together. Department chairs were relocated from the central office building to individual schools, "where they should be—facilitating and supporting the work of teachers rather than controlling and monitoring it." Positions, such as assistant superintendent for business, assistant superintendent for program and curriculum, director of elementary and secondary instruction, and subject area supervisors, were consolidated.

Attrition

Attrition had reduced the central office administration during the period of redistricting. That policy continued. In 1972, for example, there were 80 administrators for 23,000 students. As Helfrich puts it: "There were people sitting in the halls thinking of things for teachers to do. We were spending loads of money on things that didn't matter very much." In 1982–1983, there were 40 administrators in the central office; in 1994, there were 35 administrators for 9,000 students, with only 5 in the central office. This ratio is one of the lowest in New York state.

Although such changes were purposeful, it is overdramatic to say there was high reshuffling. People were not fired. If they retired, they were not replaced or jobs were combined.

Although the relocations and attrition were upsetting to the district, they were counterbalanced with a commitment to staff development. From the outset, the impending districtwide improvement process was driven by staff development. The central office was reorganized, in part, to create an administrative role for staff development—"someone to deal with the changes, which no one really knew about, yet." The person who was given that role later became the deputy superintendent. He explains that "staff development in those early years included implementing the change—not just training, but also managing the improvement initiatives."

First Steps in the Uncharted Journey

How did the administrators choose the approach it did? At an earlier stage in his career, Helfrich had been associated with the Institute for the Development of Educational Activities (I I D I E I A I), a think tank dedicated to research for the improvement of education affiliated with the Kettering Foundation in Dayton, Ohio. Helfrich tapped this network of contacts to arrange for I I I D I E I A I 's assistance in thinking through his change agenda. An I I I D I E I A I consultant recalls the chronology:

> After 2 months on the job, he called me requesting that I I I D I E I A I help the district with clinical supervision [an alternative teacher evaluation strategy]. I suggested that rather than identify a specific process, he first spend a day with the I I I D I E I A I staff and talk through the nature of the district—its history, the incidences of closings, decreases in enrollments, and the restructuring of central office—and where he wanted to go with it.

Following that meeting, a team of I I I D I E I A I staff met in Ken-Ton for a 3-day period with groups of stakeholders representing the business community, the board of education, the central office staff, and the superintendent. At this point, there was neither teacher nor union representation, which, an |I |D |E |A | consultant notes "in retrospect may not have been good judgment; however in the previous year so many grievances had been filed, that any relationship was not seen as possible at that time." Meetings lasted approximately 3 hours and focused on discussions of beliefs about the district and its strengths. As conversations moved more deeply into areas the district might focus on for improvement, the same consultant notes:

> We were advised of certain words that would not be looked on favorably. One of them was "improvement" because it implied that what they were currently doing was not absolutely the best. And it was clear that there was a great deal of pride in the schools held by the "old guard."

At the end of this series of meetings, |I |D |E |A | was charged with recommending a proposal for how the district might move forward.

The |I |D |E |A | Proposal

In June 1982, the |I |D |E |A | team presented a proposal for change to three groups in three separate meetings. One group comprised building administrators, the second comprised union leaders, and the third was the board of education. The proposal outlined a process of planned change and specifically emphasized the need for long-term commitment—5 to 7 years. A central office administrator recalls the tone of these meetings:

> [The |I |D |E |A | consultant] made a 5-minute presentation in very broad brush strokes such as, "We're looking at doing some things here that would involve change, with some great opportunities for flexibility. It will be a long-range process." He presented it lightly, as a rather broad-based contractual agreement with |I |D |E |A |. Then he asked for questions. In the building administrators' group there was absolute silence. In fact, three or four people just got up and walked out.

What did the silence mean? Why did the people up and leave? The same administrator continues:

First of all, they realized they weren't being asked to approve it, just not to block it. Secondly, if they had any questions, no one was going to be the first to ask. They just felt that the odds were that "it would go away, so why bother?"

In sharp contrast, the reaction of the executive committee of the teachers union was to raise a litany of queries about the core issues of governance, finance, and long-range planning:

This sounds awfully massive, who's going to say "yes" or "no" to this proposal? Is this going to cost a lot of money? Is it going to take away from other programs? How is this going to be supported? Is it going to be at the expense of contracts? Who's going to run it? We went through this before with Project Redesign, what makes you think that this will work? Is the superintendent even going to be here?

Despite these concerns, the union leadership agreed not to block the proposal. At the recommendation of the superintendent, the board of education entered into a consulting relationship with I I I D I E I A I. A board member explains that the contract was signed for between $20,000 and $30,000, which included the board's commitment to a 3- to 5-year plan to "make the district a better place—it was as generic as that!" Reflecting on all this later, an I I I D I E I A I consultant feels that the fact that the board stuck with that pledge may have been one of the most important factors in the process. Emphasizing the risk-taking nature of the board's 3-year commitment, the superintendent acknowledges that belief as well:

Very frankly, the SIP was a pig in a poke. It takes a lot of [courage] on the part of a board of education to be willing to do that. They can throw money down the drain . . . and at the end of 3 years . . . have nothing.

Building Consensus: The Church Meeting

The next occurrence was a 2-day team-building and brainstorming event held in a church located next to the district's central office. It later became known as "the church meeting." Facilitated by I I I D I E I A I staff, the meeting's purpose was to build consensus among the district's stakeholder groups that, in the superintendent's words, "first, we all agree that we really want to do something, and second, we commit ourselves to whatever that something is."

Between 50 and 60 people attended the meeting, representing teachers, building administrators, assistant principals, program supervisors, union representatives, members of the university and religious communities, and the board of education. Recalling that no support staff were included, a current board member observes, "Our concept of 'staff' then was different than it is today."

A second purpose of the meeting was to model the kinds of processes each school in the district would eventually use in implementing a school improvement strategy—that is, building consensus, team building, and brainstorming. Throughout the meeting, small groups took on trust-building activities designed around the following questions: What is good about this district? What is the best you can say about this district? What if you didn't have to worry about money or someone telling you "no," what would you like to do? What could you do? Everyone had an opportunity to express an opinion and to help plot the direction of change. What emerged from all this information? As simple as it may seem, participants identified the need to "build on excellence," a motto that took on great importance.

Several "background noise" factors were present in the meeting, playing out earlier historical forces and causing tension in relationships. Due to building closings, several principals were "without a home" and some had been "recycled" to other schools as program supervisors. In addition, labor contract negotiations were under way. A parent recalls the skepticism emanating from long-standing pride in the schools, as well as from the closed characteristics of the system:

> I I I D I E I A I had structured the 2 days but I don't think we followed the structure very well. We were kicking and screaming. The administrators, teachers, and probably we parents, too, all came in saying, "Why do we need someone to come in and tell us. We don't need this. Why do we need outsiders to Kenmore telling us what to do?" I think by the end, some participants, particularly the building administrators, didn't really want to be a part of it.

It was suddenly becoming clear to building administrators that it wasn't going to be business as usual. They were suspicious of this new superintendent, who was from a district with only one elementary school, one junior high and one high school, coming into a considerably larger district—a naive idealist who did not understand large systems. For many, the feeling was one of condescension, with an attitude of "this, too, shall pass; it's just another Project Redesign." It is not surprising, therefore, that there are differing views of the outcome of this event:

- An administrator viewed it as a powerful experience in team building among stakeholder groups.
- In the view of the |I |D |E |A | team, however,

> no real, earth shattering things came from that meeting. The most important thing that occurred was an increased body of people with growing awareness of the concept of school improvement, who had a common experience and a common language.

- In Helfrich's view, "as a result of that meeting everyone agreed, 'Yeah, let's get on board and get something done.' But no one really knew yet exactly what we were agreeing to. We basically agreed to a facilitated change process."
- In the opinion of a union leader, "I'm not sure |I |D |E |A | really knew the direction they were going, either. We agreed to do something different than we had been doing, but there was no commitment at that time to shared decision making."
- A board member reflects,

> This marked the beginning of quite a project! I think we were the first entire district that |I |D |E |A | ever handled. One or two schools had undertaken the process, but not an entire district. And I really believe that we wrote the script with them, because the things we started out with changed very rapidly. A lot of people forget that.

Training for District-Level Administrators

A key element in the |I |D |E |A | model is the requirement that the school improvement process be well facilitated. A district administrator explains that "there's no way the process can be implemented in an entire district without making available to the buildings support in the form of skilled facilitators at the district level."

A key event was the training of two central office administrators who were assigned to be district liaisons and who would eventually facilitate the entire SIP. The team attended |I |D |E |A |'s facilitator training in Indiana in June 1982. Throughout the training, members discussed what the next steps would be in the district and what would have to be in place. The deputy superintendent describes the experience as

> another experience with a "white board," only it was a piece of paper on a kitchen table in the college facility where the training occurred. The resulting diagram looked like it had been drawn by the nuclear physicists at Los Alamos and the Manhattan Project. Intuitively, I could grasp what the |I |D |E |A | facilitators were talking about, but the enormity of what we were about to undertake—taking 12 buildings through a change process—was something I almost didn't want to understand!

To appreciate fully the significance of this reaction and the enormity of the change effort, it is important to understand the philosophy or guiding principles and the key components of the model of change Ken-Ton adopted. That is the subject of the next chapter.

2

❖

Models of Change and the Ken-Ton Experience

In this chapter, we temporarily interrupt the Kenmore-Town of Tona-wanda Union (Ken-Ton) Free School District story to describe the | I | D | E | A | model of school improvement the district adopted and to introduce the stages the district moved through as it modified, adapted, and tailored the model to fit its needs. We follow the overview with an examination of the process in light of selected strategies of change as described in the literature.

The | I | D | E | A | Model of School Improvement

The conceptual underpinning of | I | D | E | A |'s model of planned change includes a set of assumptions about schools, school personnel, and staff development; a 10-phase systematic cycle for the continuous improvement of schools; and a mechanism—the school planning team—that enables teachers, administrators, parents, students, and community representatives to identify goals and plans collaboratively for guiding continuous improvement at the school site (| I | D | E | A |, 1993; Wood, Freeland, & Szabo, 1985; Wood & Thompson, 1980). The approach is shaped by a number of research-supported assumptions about school improvement:

1. *The target:* The unit or target of change is the school, not the district or individual staff member. Schools, however, are not independent of a school system (Berman & McLaughlin, 1978; Goodlad, 1975).
2. *The means:* The primary means of achieving improvement in student learning is not curriculum development but systematic,

21

long-range staff development based on the principles of adult learning (Joyce & Showers, 1980; Wood & Thompson, 1980).

3. *The source:* The source of improvements is research on effective schools and effective instructional practices, not intuitive judgments about interesting educational practices (Edmonds, 1979).

4. *The dissemination:* The building principal is the gatekeeper for adoption and continued use of new practices and programs in a school (Berman & McLaughlin, 1978; Edmonds, 1979; Goodlad, 1975).

5. *The process:* Planning is a proactive, long-range, systematic, vision-driven process (Edmonds, 1979; Goodlad, 1975; Sarason, 1971; Schmuck & Miles, 1971).

In the |I |D |E |A | model, these assumptions guide an ongoing, overlapping cycle of phases of continuous improvement, illustrated in Figure 2.1. They are readiness, planning, retreat, design, training, implementation, monitoring, continuous improvement, evaluation, and recycling (|I |D |E |A |, 1993).

Readiness

In the readiness phase, schools and districts examine the extent to which there is an expectation to improve and a willingness to support long-term change. Within individual schools, a planning team of 8 to 25 stakeholders who care, or should care, about the quality of the school develops an information system of research-based best practices and analyzes the school climate in terms of staff productivity and student engagement in learning.

Planning

In the planning phase, the team envisions what it wants the school to be like in 5 years, establishes specific improvement goals, and creates plans for implementation. Selected members of the team are trained as facilitators to guide the team. Through a series of structured experiences that enable members to develop the skills and trust needed to work as an effective decision-making group, the team analyzes possibilities, synthesizes information, and builds consensus. Vision is developed through the team's exposure to nine basic principles at the core of effective schools. These principles are illustrated in Figure 2.2.

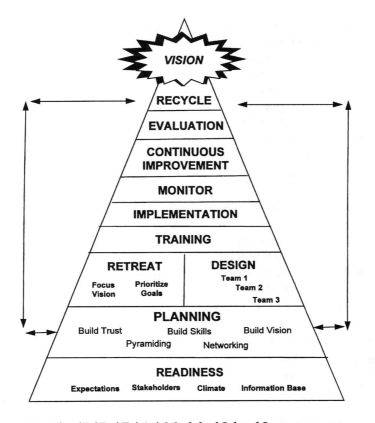

Figure 2.1. The |I |D |E |A | Model of School Improvement
SOURCE: Used by permission from Institute for Development of Educational Activities
(|I |D |E |A |, 1993).

To develop broad ownership in the work of the team, planning team members form pyramid groups composed of five to seven peers. Team members meet with these groups to keep them informed and to elicit reactions to the work of the planning team. Networking systems are developed across schools to provide the opportunity for building facilitators to share plans, successes, and problems.

Retreat and Design

In the retreat and design phases, planning team members meet during a 2- or 3-day retreat to specify goals for improvement and decide which programs and practices will achieve these goals. Follow-

---

1. Education is increasingly used to prepare students for successful life transitions.

2. Schools make every effort to link students with appropriate community resources that could make a positive contribution to the student's education.

3. Students become increasingly self-directed through planned leading to self-educating adulthood.

4. Schools explicitly teach and reward the agreed upon values of the school and community.

5. Parents are expected to be active participants in the education of their children.

6. Each student pursues excellence in an area of his or her own choosing.

7. Everyone affected by a decision is involved directly or representatively in the making of it.

8. Schools strive to integrate the interdependent educational efforts of the home, school, and community.

9. Every participant involved in educating youth, models the role of learner.

Figure 2.2. Nine Principles of Education
SOURCE: Used by permission from Institute for Development of Educational Activities
(I I ID I E I A I, 1993).

ing this goal-setting session, members of the planning team join with new stakeholders to form design teams that identify implementation plans that will move the school toward its goals. Their written plans include details for training, timelines for implementation, formative and summative evaluation data, and a strategy for obtaining commitment from the school faculty, central office administrators, and parents. When the design is completed, it is submitted to the planning team for review, revision, and approval.

Training and Implementation

In the training and implementation phases, team members work with the principal and other administrators to get faculty support and to initiate inservice training. Training plans are implemented that focus on the knowledge, attitudes, and skills needed to implement new practices at the school site.

Monitoring, Continuous Improvement, Evaluation

In the monitoring phase, formal and informal measures are used to determine if the plan is in place. The information gained is used, in the continuous improvement phase, to modify ongoing implementation efforts. During the evaluation phase, information is gathered to determine if desired results were achieved—for example, increased teacher and student satisfaction, lower drop-out rates, improved attendance, higher student achievement.

Recycle

In the recycle phase, as members of the planning team and design teams step down to be replaced by new stakeholders, more and more members of the school community gain understanding of the process of guiding school improvement.

Key to the successful implementation of the process is the training of facilitators in each building to guide a team through the cycle. The group receiving facilitator training generally consists of at least one parent, administrator, teacher, and a support staff member. The training requires two workshops, held 4 to 6 months apart, that focus on developing group facilitation skills such as inclusion, team building, brainstorming, and consensus seeking. Central office leaders are also trained to provide support to building teams and to create possibilities for networking among schools. In Ken-Ton, all administrators received facilitator training; this practice continues to be the case.

Ken-Ton's Cycle of Improvement

In Ken-Ton, the implementation of the |I |D |E |A | model evolved through four distinct periods that we have labeled stages. The first stage followed the period of downsizing and retrenchment described in Chapter 1. Morale was low and relations among teachers, administrators, schools, and the community were distinctly adversarial. The new superintendent responded to the crisis with a program to revitalize the district. Although Helfrich calls this the *stage of conceptualization,* it entailed more than that. It required conceptualizing a vision for the district, then moving quickly to ensure that the new

organizational structures and participative processes prescribed by the
|I |D |E |A | model were put in place districtwide.

High expectations challenged each school in the district to form a
planning team, to train facilitators, and to complete the readiness,
planning, and retreat phases of the |I |D |E |A | cycle by the end of
the first year. The intent was to "let those who wanted to move, move;
then let others catch up." By the fall of 1983, each school had met the
challenge. Throughout the rest of this very volatile stage, which lasted
4 years (from 1982 to 1986), schools moved through the design and
inservice training phases at different paces.

The second stage was one of alignments, in which district members' concerns for the protection of self-interests moved closer to a
common purpose. When participants refer to this stage, they talk
about it as *buy-in*. It too lasted approximately 4 years (from 1986 to
1990). By the end of this stage, all the school planning teams had com-
pleted the implementation and monitoring phases of the |I |D |E |A |
cycle.

Participants refer to the third period, which lasted 2 years (from
1990 to 1992), as the *stage of ownership*. When people saw what could
be accomplished, they expressed excitement about the future, were
more willing to participate in the improvement process, and were more
open to assessing what they had been doing. It was during this period
that the district applied for and won the Excelsior award. In so doing,
it accomplished the continuous improvement and evaluation phases
of the |I |D |E |A | cycle.

The fourth stage was perceived as a *focus on quality*. The award
application process required the district to examine and document the
results it had achieved. Self-assessment set the agenda for a shift in
emphasis from school improvement to a districtwide focus on quality. This shift sent the district spiraling into the recycle phase of the
|I |D |E |A | model.

Models of Planned Organizational Change

We have used the concept of stages as a template that, when
applied to the Ken-Ton experience, provides a framework for organizing how participants understood and interpreted the historical
processes and events through which the school improvement program (SIP) evolved. These participant-identified periods invite fur-

ther examination against the theoretical stages described in several models of planned change found in the literature. We've selected three familiar models for comparison. First is Lewin's (1947) action research model; second are the models that identify types or levels of change; and third are the models associated with continuous improvement.

Lewin's Model of Action Research

Lewin (1947) uses a concept of force field analysis to identify driving and restraining forces acting on organizational change and to prompt a search for ways of overcoming resistance. He describes a three-phase process of how change takes place: (1) unfreezing, or overcoming resistance by reducing the negative forces through new or disconfirming information; (2) moving, or mobilizing commitment by changing attitudes, values, structure, feelings and behaviors; and (3) refreezing, or institutionalizing change by reaching a new status quo with support mechanisms to maintain the desired behavior.

In Ken-Ton's first stage of conceptualization, low staff and community morale and the accompanying need for improved student achievement were forces driving the direction of change. Restraining forces included fear of change, complacency, perceived lack of resources, conflicts, and inertia. Applying Lewin's (1947) prescription, Superintendent Helfrich, his senior administrators, and external consultants can be considered change agents who, according to the model, overcame resistance and mobilized commitment by encouraging the participation of those affected by the change.

Other actions consistent with the action research model are represented in Ken-Ton's second stage—implementing the change slowly, training staff in the skills and techniques required by school improvement, and supporting early first change attempts to increase involvement. The |I |D |E |A | approach mobilized commitment by requiring the design of mechanisms to maintain open and frequent communication and by creating a climate of experimentation and innovation. By getting people to work together on projects, the planning teams broke down traditional barriers among parents, teachers, administrators, and support staff. It was no longer "us and them." Through a variety of techniques such as brainstorming and problem solving, the teams created synergy among school personnel, helping them feel they made a difference.

By the end of the third stage (starting the refreezing), change had been institutionalized. The planning teams, for example, broke down and then rebuilt the information, influence, and affective links among staff in each school. A whole new set of linkages among people was created that cut across traditional functions and encouraged collaboration on planning directions for both schools and the district.

Types (or Levels) of Change

A related avenue of exploration is the type of change the SIP achieved. Ways of understanding events are guided by organizing frameworks often called *paradigms* (Kuhn, 1970, Weick, 1979). They are also referred to as *schemata* (Bartunek & Moch, 1987; Markus & Zajonc, 1985), *frames* (Goffman, 1974), or *theory in use* (Argyris & Schon, 1978). Another set of academics has classified change attempts as three generalized types (Argyris & Schon, 1978; Golembiewski, Billingsley, & Yeager, 1976; Watzlawick, Weakland, & Fisch, 1974).

Type one, or first-order, changes are consistent with an existing paradigm or interpretation of events. Increased skill in participative decision making based on agreement that participation is valuable is an example of first-order change.

Type two, or second-order, changes modify an existing paradigm in a particular direction. One paradigm is phased out as another is phased in. Practices that foster shared decision making but that cause middle managers (such as building principals) to feel that their prerogatives or jobs are threatened exemplify an impetus for second-order change. That is, the implementation of the practice requires a change in the existing order of the administrators and the organization.

The third type, third-order change, unlike the first two that result in incremental modifications, is frame breaking (Tushman & Nadler, 1982). This level of change results in redefinition of an organization's mission, changing the distribution of power, altering patterns of interaction, and adding new leadership.

Ken-Ton's school improvement initiative may have begun as first-order change, but it eventually accomplished second-order or even frame-breaking change. It resulted in the creation of new organizational structures to accommodate the process of decentralized decision making. It was, therefore, quite different from the district's old operating norms, where historically decisions about change were made in the central office.

Continuous Improvement Models of Change

A more recent line of inquiry into the nature of organizations and how they should be changed is associated with the quality movement. Total quality management (TQM) is both a philosophy and a set of practices that use principles of leadership, quantitative methods, systems thinking, and empowerment to improve an organization's ability to meet the needs and requirements of its clients or customers continuously. Total quality programs emphasize the responsibilities and accountability of all employees for achieving client satisfaction through continuous improvement of the quality of an organization's processes, products, and services. This often interferes with long-standing departmental monopolies over functions perceived to be a source of power and career status. To deal effectively with those powerful traditions, TQM requires that top management create a supportive organizational structure. To the extent that TQM requires the restructuring of organizations to integrate the efforts of all groups in achieving customer satisfaction (Feigenbaum, 1983), it is a model of change.

The conceptual underpinnings of TQM are described in the philosophies of Deming (1982, 1986), Juran (1974), Crosby (1979), Feigenbaum (1983), Ishikawa (1985), Imai (1986), and Tagushi (1986). Of the seven, the principal model for guiding the process of change and continuous improvement throughout an entire organization is the Deming Cycle, or the Plan-Do-Check-Act Cycle (PDCA; Gabor, 1990). The PDCA cycle is a vehicle for focusing every organizational function on defining and refining the requirements of customers and requiring the constant cooperation of all departments. The four steps in the PDCA cycle involve (1) planning what is to be done, (2) doing or carrying out the plan, (3) checking to see whether the plan worked as intended, (4) and acting on what worked or what did not work. This cycle applies to virtually all levels and functions in an organization (Gabor, 1990).

The analysis inherent in the PDCA continuum is the basis for policy deployment, which provides a structure for continuous improvement. Policy deployment is based on three elements: top management's philosophical commitment to the concept of continuous improvement, middle management's ability to standardize improvements throughout the organization, and the ability of the entire organization to innovate on the basis of those standards and improvements (Imai, 1986).

Holmes (1992) identifies developmental stages in the quality implementation process. She describes a continuum of phases (Stages 1 and 2, Stage 3, and Stage 4) involving six factors: the source of pressure to implement TQM practices, employee perceptions, ownership of the improvement process, evidence of resistance, observable responses, and critical tasks. In the early phase (Stages 1 and 2), top management is the source of pressure to implement TQM. Employees perceive TQM as a fad, an activity not integrated into daily work processes. Ownership of the process is located in pockets of enthusiastic supporters but, in Stage 3, it gradually expands to include middle management and hourly workers.

Widespread resistance in Stages 1 and 2 takes the form of defensiveness in front-line managers and wait-and-see attitudes in middle managers who, in Stage 3, test the system and retain autocratic behaviors. Observable responses move from frustration, in Stages 1 and 2, to emerging systemic changes, particularly in compensation and appraisal systems, in Stage 3. Critical tasks evolve from identifying appropriate champions of the change in the first phase (Stages 1 and 2) to breaking down barriers and clarifying roles in the second phase (Stage 3). In the phase of maturity, Stage 4, the source of pressure shifts from top management alone to include support from lower levels. Employees perceive quality as a process, an overarching goal; ownership shifts to the local division level; resistance is evidenced in the confusion of middle managers about roles and expectations; observable responses include effective use of resources; and the critical tasks are building trust and demonstrating values.

There is supportive evidence of each of these TQM phases in Ken-Ton's district-identified stages of change. In response to the crisis of downsizing during the stage of conceptualization, the board of education and the superintendent were the sources of pressure to create a vision for the district and to adopt the |I |D |E |A | model for school improvement that specified the tactics and strategies for responding to the demands of the community. Staff, particularly building principals, viewed the improvement initiative as an extra activity not integrated into the daily work of their schools. Throughout the stages of conceptualization and buy-in, ownership of improvement efforts was located in clusters of enthusiastic supporters of school planning teams. By the end of the stage of ownership, however, everyone was aware that the |I |D |E |A | improvement cycle had become standard practice.

Widespread resistance in the early stages took the form of wait-and-see attitudes in some building administrators, who tested the new system and either retained control or minimized the role of their own school planning team. Observable responses in Ken-Ton moved from small individual improvement projects in the first stage to emerging systemic changes in training, compensation, and appraisal systems in the second and third stages. The critical tasks evolved from creating mechanisms for building trust and demonstrating values in the first stage to clarifying the role and supporting the improvement projects of school planning teams in the second stage. Finally, in Stage 3 the source of pressure shifted from the superintendent and his senior administrators to include support from all levels of the district's staff. The entire school community perceived continuous improvement as an overarching goal and ownership was located at the building or department level. Resistance was still somewhat evidenced in the skepticism of some staff about the district's emphasis on state and national awards. By the end of the third stage, however, the district's participants were more concerned with improving the effectiveness of planning teams; the critical tasks that were identified were integrating building and district-level priorities and improving methods of data collection.

Taking a Second Look at Planned Change

Models of planned change rely heavily on rational assumptions of cause and effect. They imply that change can be made successfully if we define objectives clearly, plan sufficiently, control the process carefully, monitor progress systematically, and assess outcomes objectively. But in the case of the Lewin (1947) model, for example, how long does the refreezing last? For Weisbord (1987), the concept falls apart as relentless, unpredictable swings in communities, governments, economies, and technologies cause perpetual transition—a state described by Vaill (1991) as "permanent white water." The cycles tumble so fast that whatever is refrozen may last only weeks or months instead of years.

Models of continuous improvement also suggest that change can be planned and carried out in a rational fashion. The philosophy of TQM is based on rational thinking, and the four-step sequence of the Deming cycle is clearly a straightforward problem-solving process. Such models evolved from general systems theory (Boulding, 1964;

Von Bertalanffy, 1975), which emphasizes the search for laws that govern order in a system's environment.

Because orderliness can quickly change to disorder, it is the leader's role to find a balance between the order of the organization and of the environment (Leifer, 1989). But according to Quinn (1985), in the organizations from which models of change have been derived, the events that precipitated changes—typically recessions and financial crises—were not planned. This suggests that organizations are not likely to be changed merely through careful planning. According to Deal (1985), planning works only in the short term:

> Specifying objectives may induce a temporary vision to bolster confidence. Planning may implicitly facilitate sharing the vision. Planning task forces and meetings may help create shared meaning. Reports may reduce ambiguity and symbolize that changes are on the right track. But when new changes begin to encroach on the task at hand, leaders rush quickly to restore order and return to the main agenda (p. 324).

As in the Lewin (1947) action research approach, the improvement process may be preempted at any step in the model by permanent white water, which can also be described as the "edge of chaos."

The approach of planned change proposes the use of orderly strategies in a disorderly world. It is not entirely equal to the challenge of explaining how change actually takes place, how order is created out of disorder, or how an organization such as Ken-Ton became expert at dealing with the turbulence of permanent white water and was able to survive the vicissitudes of planned and unplanned change while growing and developing.

New Rules:
Discoveries About Chaos

The assumptions of planned change are being challenged by new models and new rules. In a model suggested by quantum theory for example, change occurs abruptly and discontinuously in surprises and quantum leaps. According to Wheatley (1992), at work, although we can't observe it, is a system of interactions creating the conditions that lead to a sudden jump.

This model more closely approximates the Ken-Ton experience than do models of planned change. Rather than finding order created through long-range planning, the Ken Ton case reflects order as emerging from instability, through experimentation and trial and error. Ken-Ton's journey through school improvement resulted not from a single vision formulated at the top of the organization, but from a complex intertwining of events and people. The designers had no clear picture of a future state. Instead they were driven by dissatisfactions and disruptions arising in the present state in which they continuously operated.

In the unfolding picture of Ken-Ton, you will see that implementation strategies were just in time, supported by investment in staff development focused on expanding the skills of staff. Such strategies required the ability to do a quick study and to trust in intuitions.

The new science of chaos has developed powerful descriptions of the ways complex systems cope effectively with uncertainty and rapid change (Gleick, 1987; Senge, 1992; Waldrop, 1992; Wheatley, 1992). The new rules suggest that a system, such as a school district, cannot be understood simply by examining parts and looking for cause-and-effect links that are close together in time and space. Thinking has to proceed in terms of whole systems, their interconnections, and the patterns they generate.

In the chapters that follow, we resume the chronology of the Ken-Ton school improvement initiative. At times the relationships described may appear to be best understood as cause and effect, but the links between actions and results are infinitely more complicated than such linear relations might indicate. To understand the subtleties of the implementation of the school improvement process requires seeing the whole system as it both generated and lived the experience.

The SIP moved through four stages, each with identifiable tasks to be carried out, processes or strategies through which those tasks were accomplished, a climate surrounding task accomplishment, challenges or obstacles to be addressed, and outcomes driving the process to the next stage of development. In the ensuing chapters, our intent is to capture in participants' words the details of the unfolding of these events, the gradual accumulation of change, and the overall behavior of the system. In Part II, our challenge is to move beyond the innumerable and fragmented events to the whole—to appreciate how things moved and changed as a coherent entity. As the story unfolds, we encourage the reader to take note of examples of confusion, ill-structured problems, continuing contention, and other such symptoms of a system moving through chaos into synthesis, which will be the subject of Chapter 11.

3

Stage 1 (1982–1986)

Conceptualizing a Change Strategy

In Chapter 1, we examined the historical forces leading to the initiation of the school improvement program (SIP) and the first steps in the implementation process. We summarize them here briefly to provide a link to the first stage of its implementation. Following a period in the 1970s of massive layoffs, declining staff morale, and parental dissatisfaction—all the result of declining enrollments—the board of education recognized the need to counter the decline with an emphasis on improving the quality of student learning. In 1981, a new superintendent, Jack Helfrich, challenged the district to become involved in a comprehensive school improvement effort. He began by reducing the number of central office administrators and creating a new administrative role for staff development.

In 1982, the board of education made a long-term commitment to a facilitated change process, beginning with the training of a team of district-level administrators. Thus began a process of decentralized decision making quite different from the way the Kenmore-Town of Tonawanda Union (Ken-Ton) Free School District traditionally had operated. Historically, decisions about change were made in the central office. In this and the next three chapters, participants describe the four major stages through which Ken-Ton's unique experience of school improvement evolved as it adapted the |I |D |E |A | school-based approach to an entire district. Each chapter is structured to convey: participant perceptions of the tasks for each stage; the sequence of processes and events through which the tasks were accomplished; staff attitudes and feelings about the climate, or what it was like to be involved in the events of each stage; the challenges to or obstacles in the way of task accomplishment; and outcomes that led to the next stage of the SIP.

Building the Agenda:
The Tasks of Stage 1

Something was to be done.

How do you begin a school improvement program? As Superintendent Helfrich describes it, the district's slogan, "Build on Excellence," (an outcome of the church event) represented agreement among stake holders that "something was to be done" to create a more positive learning environment for students. The first step, then, was to concep-tualize what was to be done. As Helfrich recalls it, "We were going to have shared decision making. We were going to have decentralization. To do that we needed building planning teams with trained facilitators, who could deal with visionary things." That statement identifies the agenda the district was to pursue for initiating the SIP.

Task I: Establish Expectations for Change

It will be done.

The board of education's commitment to the school improvement process and the superintendent's determination to make it happen established overt expectations for change. There was no grand master plan, however. Instead, a more subtle expectation targeted individual schools as units of change and set in motion a process that all schools followed.

- All building administrators would receive training.
- All buildings would designate facilitators to be trained and would form school planning teams.
- All planning teams would proceed through a cycle of four or five awareness meetings, ending with a day-long planning retreat to establish long-range goals.

An administrator notes that the message was simply, "It will be done."

Task 2: Demonstrate Trust and Commitment

Treat us like professionals.

Staff development was a priority from the beginning. The board set aside a sizable amount of money for staff development because it "really felt . . . teachers needed to see new things were happening." An administrator estimates that everything done in the first year to support the improvement initiative probably cost less than $100,000, but if people knew that it cost even that much, "it probably would have triggered a revolution because there was no trust."

Teachers perceived support of staff development as a demonstration of the district's commitment to change. Recalling a point in the process where schools with visions in place submitted budgets to the central office, a teacher says, "That was different! The first thing I ever worked on where there was money!"

Risk taking in contract negotiations also signaled the district's commitment. A union leader relates the importance to teachers of being treated as professionals:

> The idea of informal negotiations was broached, and both sides [were] willing to sit down and talk about settling. That worked well . . . and we've done that for the last 10 years. That was another commitment that they were going to treat you like a professional person.

Task 3: Provide a Mechanism for Renewal

A good way for people to see results quickly.

Providing resources and support for each building to form planning teams and begin the cycle of awareness meetings and retreats prescribed by the I I I D I E I A I model set in motion the beginnings of a mechanism for change. The first 3 or 4 years was a period of experimenting with the formation and operations of the teams. Challenges arose related to communicating the team's purpose or role and its composition. We describe those challenges later in this chapter.

During the next 4 years, these three tasks were accomplished through a sequence of processes and events that required developing new skills, attitudes, and commitments to new behaviors.

Chronology of the
Stage 1 Events and Processes

During the first year of the SIP, six major processes and events contributed to conceptualizing a districtwide improvement strategy for Ken-Ton. These are summarized in Table 3.1. A close examination of the events makes it clear that Ken-Ton's SIP was largely driven by staff development.

Year 1 (1982–1983)

We're really going to do this.

Because the unit of change was the school, clearly there was a need for principals, as key instructional leaders, to understand the school improvement process and to acquire the leadership skills necessary to support and guide it. Early on, all principals, program supervisors, and central office staff participated in a 2-year program that used collegial support groups as the means through which principals improved their competence related to school improvement.

The Principals' Inservice Program called for groups of 6 to 10 building administrators to meet monthly in 4-hour sessions facilitated by the district facilitators to explore problems in a climate of trust and mutual assistance. That was the plan. But there were surprises. Resistance was one surprise that sparked a variety of interpretations by those who had to deal with it. We describe the program in detail here because it illustrates lessons to be learned about the timing, sequencing, and structuring of initial events in the change process.

TABLE 3.1 Summary of the Ken-Ton School Improvement Process

Year	Date	Processes and Events
		The Environment Prior to the Initiative
	1955–1967	Stable leadership, community pride Student population peaked at 23,000
	1968–1981	Population declined to 8,000 students Buildings were reduced from 28 to 12
	1970s	Redistricting, layoffs, declining morale, contentious labor-management and community relations State and national trends to reform
	1981	New superintendent began reorganization Board adopted I I I D I E I A I model of planned change
		Stage 1: Conceptualization
1	1982–1983	Principals' inservice training launched the school improvement program Computer literacy training districtwide Union-sponsored research and dissemination training project School planning teams formed, began I I I D I E I A I planning cycle Planning team facilitator training initiated District-level planning team formed
2	1983–1984	Administrator support groups formed Clinical supervision adopted
3	1984–1985	Madison Six Team established 4MAT turnkey-style training delivery districtwide School planning team retreats and facilitator training continued Networking with other districts
4	1985–1986	Learning Styles training districtwide District planning retreats extended to all stakeholders Mentor program conceptualized

(continued)

TABLE 3.1 (Continued)

Year	Date	Processes and Events

Stage 2: Buy-In

5	1986–1987	Planning teams began process of monitoring
6	1987–1988	Mentor program implemented
		Support staff planning teams formed
7	1988–1989	Teacher Center established
		First State School of Excellence Award received
8	1989–1990	Career credit professional development program instituted

Stage 3: Ownership

9	1990–1991	Cutting-edge labor-management contracts designed
		Hiring process decentralized
		Support staff involvement increased
		First National School of Excellence Award received
		Business-community linkages expanded
10	1991–1992	Intervention component of Mentor Program accepted
		Career credit program extended to support staff
		Shared decision making formalized in union contracts
		Multicultural curricular focus
		First district to receive New York State Excelsior Award for quality in education

Stage 4: Focus on Quality

11	1992–1993	
12	1993–1994	
		Focus on learning and instruction renewed
		Need to reconcile district priorities with site-based planning recognized
		Seven of thirteen schools had attained National School of Excellence Awards
		Superintendent and deputy announced retirements

The Principals' Inservice Program

To kick off the program in the summer of 1982, Ken-Ton hosted a national workshop conducted by |I |D |E |A | consultants. The program provided a forum in which the Ken-Ton team of two district facilitators and the superintendent, together with |I |D |E |A | facilitator-trainees from around the country, practiced recently acquired facilitation skills under the guidance of consultants. During the workshop, the facilitator-trainees guided Ken-Ton's administrator-students through sample activities they might encounter in the Principals' Inservice Program.

As with the church meeting, there were "noise" factors. The superintendent recalled that there was almost open rebellion. The notion of shared decision making and decentralization threatened the principals' power. There was also the attitude that "We've been through this before. We're already good. Three years and he'll be gone!" An |I |D |E |A | consultant recalls a slightly different scenario: "The administrators' association was upset that the superintendent presumed (administrators) would be available . . . in the summer. They resented the expectation, told him so, and asked about this nonsense of improving schools." The superintendent allowed administrators to "hit hard." He listened and responded, not by using power nor by reprimanding, but by giving rational reasons and his own perceptions. Some observers later acknowledged that this took courage, "more than most leaders have."

A district facilitator provides a third perspective, noting that in a meeting immediately following the church meeting earlier in the summer, the superintendent reassigned half of the elementary principals to different buildings. Their reaction was predictable and understandable: "At 4:00 in the afternoon you have us stick around and tell us we're going to have different buildings in September. What is that saying about empowerment, involvement?"

Nor were administrators told that they would be busy over the summer. When did they find out about the Principals' Inservice Program? About 10 days before the event was to take place. A district facilitator explains that the message to 40 administrators was

be there! So, they came, not knowing anything about was going to happen to them . . . and then found out they were going to be a class for "student-facilitators!" Of course, some of the activities [in the workshop] overlapped the things they had been through at the church meeting, which only added to their irritation!

Skepticism and resistance continued to color the tone of the administrators' inservice groups, which met 1 day per month for a year to work on planning skills, to help each other solve immediate problems, and to prepare for supporting improvement projects in individual schools.

The program did not go smoothly for all. A district facilitator explains that three groups "sailed through" the program. The assistant principals and program supervisors thought they had "died and gone to heaven" because they had a day a month away from discipline problems and being told what to do, and there was the opportunity to philosophize, generate ideas, and support one another. On the other hand, a central office group resented being there, perceiving it as a waste of time. This group was not "about to argue with the superintendent," however. For the principals, it was like trying to get the "Arabs and the Israelis together . . . it was a long battle!"

According to the same facilitator, what eventually turned the inservice program around was the realization that the administrators were hurting one another, not the administration. He recalls a breakthrough discussion of a group expectations survey in which individual participants rated their group on 10 statements such as, "Suppose someone in this group has said something you don't understand. How many others in the group do you think are interested in knowing when you do not understand something he has said?" Or "Suppose you just presented a difficult concept to the group and someone humiliated you. About how many people in the group do you think would speak up for you or would really care?"

Out of 12 people, only 2 or 3 indicated they felt safe in the first situation or respected the other person in the second. The group concluded that, "nothing they're asking us to do is as bad as what we're doing to each other!" From that point on, the resistance changed to an uneasy acceptance that "they're serious. We're really going to do this!" From a facilitator's perspective those meetings were "like playing ambassador to Israel and the PLO." When asked to explain his persistence, as well as his own source of support, the facilitator gives us a glimpse of the strength of commitment and endurance required of those who were champions of the change:

> I guess I had one failing and that is I believed in the school improvement program. As it unfolded, I really thought that there was no reason why it couldn't work for all of us. It might take some time, but we could actually do it. And every little hurdle that you had to cross was just that much easier the next time. After a while the pain threshold grows and you can really handle a lot!

The same facilitator paints a poignant picture of the lessons learned from the experimental, trial-and-error nature of the first year of the SIP. Speculating that the negativity may have been created by the timing of events as well as the way the Principals' Inservice Program was handled, he reflects:

> Conceptually, it seemed logical to prepare administrators to take a school planning team through the improvement process. But there were problems with the strategy. It was unbelievably structured. You can imagine going through literally a 6-hour day of structured activities!

With regard to sequence, he explains that the principals were not informed until November about forming school planning teams (SPTs) and taking them through a cycle of meetings. Their first task was to choose two facilitators to receive training, along with themselves, one month later.

It was time for reaction, and reaction the planners certainly got! The principals' response was, "Training for what? You want me to get two other people to do this and you can't even describe what they're doing?" The facilitator admits that "we couldn't describe it, really. We had only just been through facilitator training ourselves!"

This facilitator's final assessment of the contention and conflict surrounding the first major training event of the improvement initiative provides an important insight into the strategy of introducing change:

There were a lot of technical errors. You can have all the right ideas and still make a shambles of it in terms of how it was done. It took a fair amount of "undoing" to get back on the track of school planning teams.

What would he do differently? He would "begin with a workshop or two and then move into half-day meetings, less structured and less frequent, with the group developing the meeting agendas."

The Training of SPT Facilitators

A second important process in the first year was the training of staff in each building to form and to guide their SPTs through the improvement process. Two district facilitators and two |I |D |E |A | consultants conducted the first phase on-site throughout the spring of 1983.

Training Content and Design. The first phase of the training provided facilitators with skills to lead their teams through the phases of readiness and planning. Content focused on developing an understanding of change theory and learning to plan and conduct the initial awareness workshops necessary to get stakeholders' commitment to a school improvement plan.

The facilitator-trainees were formed into a SPT that worked through meeting agendas and typical activities, much as a real planning team in a school would. They learned techniques to facilitate team building, brainstorming, problem solving, and consensus building and to understand the role of the process observer and his or her contributions to group improvement. They also learned how to interpret educational trends and use |I |D |E |A |'s Nine Principles of Education as tools for gathering data to identify discrepancies between their vision of an ideal school and their own school's current state. Finally, they learned about pyramid groups as a way to inform the school community about the team's activities and to build support for the improvement initiative.

Subsequent training addressed the retreat and design phases of the school improvement cycle (described in Chapter 2). The facilitator-trainees learned the skills necessary to guide a retreat in which their teams would identify indicators or outcome statements that describe their ideal school in 5 years. They also learned how to select and charge a design team with developing a 5-year school improvement plan so that it would include first-year program objectives, inservice training plans to support implementation, a plan for getting commitment to the design from the school community, and a plan for formative and summative evaluation.

Participants' perceptions of the training ranged from seeing it as a waste of time to appreciating its value as a critical step in the process. As a board member explains, "once we formed our own team, it was very obvious that they needed a process . . . you were never going to get anything done unless you knew what process to use."

Formation of SPTs

During 1982–1983, each building in the district formed an SPT and began the cycle of awareness meetings (four or five per team) followed by a planning retreat. Despite a common process, team formation evolved differently for each building. Although principals knew they needed to form teams, the lack of criteria made the initial selection of team members difficult. One principal explains that in his school, members were invited rather than elected: "We were told to ask positive people. So, not really knowing what the SPT was and where we were heading . . . I felt it was my job to . . . purposefully select people." Other schools viewed it in terms of balance: "We think in terms of identifying parents, teachers, and other staff members who . . . have a strength we need . . . or certain ideas about how a school should be run. You don't want everybody thinking the same way."

Initially, the cycle of meetings was an equally diverse process across schools. Although team meetings occurred monthly on school time and staff were released from their classes to attend, for many it was a struggle to make the meetings productive:

> In the beginning, the groups were a bit stand-offish. Teachers felt that this is their turf. They were professionals. They knew what they were doing. Why did they need to ask outsiders? Even parents were shy at the beginning. They would sit on one side of the table together and were afraid to say anything because they didn't want to antagonize professional people.

A teacher remembers that faculty did not have a lot of trust in the teams, and when asked to be visionary, "they didn't have visions, they had gripes!" In a school where the process went quite smoothly, another teacher recalls that the team spent an entire year on the nine principles (see Figure 2.2, this volume, page 24):

> We went over them word by word. Many were difficult to understand. We brainstormed and talked about what each meant. At the end of the year we had a retreat. For 3 days we rehashed each principle and settled on Number 3 as our focus. Number 3 reads: "Students become increasingly self-directed through planned activities leading to self-educating adulthood." The next step was to have a design team decide how to make that a reality in the school.

As this formation process played out, a key element was providing support to those trained to facilitate teams. Therefore, an important third process came about in the first year of the improvement initiative. This was the formation of district-level support groups.

Formation of Support Groups for Team Facilitators

District-level facilitators continually met with building administrators and team facilitators, providing support and assistance in planning meeting agendas, debriefing team meetings, and providing process feedback from a district perspective. An I I D I E I A I consultant explains that the role was "a key and sophisticated one. It had to do with ensuring that a districtwide perspective was maintained; not rubber stamping what each school is doing, rather asking each school to stretch it's own goals in the direction of district goals." Out of this process evolved the mutual support groups for building facilitators in which they could share ideas about what was working in each building. These groups became a primary vehicle for the dissemination of information across the district.

Districtwide Staff Development

In addition to the support provided by district-level facilitators, two significant events further demonstrated the district's commitment to school improvement: its support of computer literacy training and a teacher association project known as Research and Dissemination. Both occurred in 1982. A union leader explains that these two projects demonstrated that, "they really mean what they're talking about. It was a major commitment . . . to inservice education."

In response to a proposal that all teachers be computer literate, the district provided the money for substitutes, which enabled 640 teachers to receive four half days of computer skills training. Concurrently, Ken-Ton was selected to participate in an American Federation of Teachers' project aimed at the dissemination of educational research. Two teachers from each building were paid by the district to attend union-sponsored training to become "educational linkers." Their function was to disseminate to their colleagues research on classroom management techniques such as monitoring time on tasks, organizing a classroom for efficiency, dealing with at-risk students, and scheduling content. The district also supported the dissemination of techniques through inservice programs held independently or in conjunction with faculty meetings in each building.

To summarize, by the end of the first year of implementation, five major strategies had launched the school improvement effort. Building administrators and team facilitators had been trained in school improvement strategies; building planning teams had been formed, as had support groups for facilitators; and districtwide training demonstrated the district's commitment to change.

Year 2 (1983–1984)

A different kind of accountability.

As a result of the research and dissemination project, "people were once again talking about instruction." In a very natural next step, both teachers and principals learned and practiced peer clinical supervision.

Peer Clinical Supervision

Peer clinical supervision is a consultation model that uses classroom observation by peers to help colleagues incorporate new instructional strategies into their practice. A person to be observed identifies classroom practices he or she would like to improve. Two or three faculty members who understand what the observee is trying to improve complete an observation and provide feedback, which is limited to the areas identified by the person observed. The observee may choose to hear about other things observers notice, but only by invitation (Goldhammer, 1969; Withall & Wood, 1979; Wood & Neil, 1976). There is no paper trail, no summary of the lesson or the feedback session. The only documentation is the date that it occurred.

A program of clinical supervision began in Ken-Ton in 1983 to ensure the classroom influence of improvement strategies. As with the case of computer training, the district provided the resources to pay substitutes so that teams comprising an administrator and three or four teachers from each school could receive two and a half days of training. Although it began as a pilot project to introduce building administrators to the concept, ultimately more than 200 people were trained. A union leader explains the model's attraction:

> The opportunity to be exposed to a colleague's classroom, to be responsible for commenting on one another's work, and receiving feedback on one's own work had seldom been talked about directly as part of union business—and now here it was, but it came from "the other side." It enabled us to approach the profession of teaching in a way we hadn't been encouraged before.

Many in the district consider clinical supervision to be a benchmark in the SIP. It provided a safe arena for teachers to debate instructional and classroom performance issues and to retain control of the feedback process. It expanded the thinking and philosophy of the union to include the concept of challenging its own members. And it provided a different kind of accountability for administrators—that of true dialogue. It was later one of a series of alternatives to traditional performance evaluation by administrators and was the catalyst for a variety of shared decision mechanisms that became hallmarks of the SIP.

Years 3 and 4 (1984–1986)

We can make a difference!

During the third and fourth years, as SPTs addressed their schools' initial priorities, districtwide planning retreats became annual events to clarify expectations and identify the district's direction for the coming year. Leaders of all planning teams as well as community stakeholders attended. The retreats aligned support for the improvement initiative and for establishing expectations for continuous improvement. A district leader explains:

> We began to form a habit of going into things—about one a year—with huge expectations. The first year it was SPTs. The second year it was clinical supervision . . . and then we started to hold retreats to clarify what the expectations were and to generate support and enthusiasm.

In addition, the district reached out in networking arrangements nationwide. A board member explains the strategy:

> At a conference where we were presenting a workshop with | I | D | E | A |, we met districts from Kansas and Colorado that were just starting their school improvement process. Later, our boards met and we exchanged staff. That caused a lot of people to feel rejuvenated as professionals.

The Madison Six Team and Learning Styles

These 2 years also marked the beginning of a staff-initiated effort to improve instructional effectiveness and established the precedent for the way staff development would continue to be conducted in the district. In the spring of 1985, six of the district's "educational linkers" attended an | I | D | E | A | workshop in Madison, Wisconsin, on current educational trends. The topic was the 4-MAT Teaching Model (McCarthy, 1980, 1985), a curriculum delivery method based on the concept of learning styles (Kolb, 1974, 1985) and research on right-left brain preferences (Sperry, 1973).

The purpose of the 4-MAT system is to raise teachers' awareness of four distinct learning styles that students tend to adopt. Rather than segregating learners on the basis of their preferred style, 4-MAT advocates an instructional cycle that provides experiences in each style for all students in a classroom.

Ken-Ton's participants (who had dubbed themselves the Madison Six) were convinced. One member of the team recalls that on the last day of the 5-day program, the group got together and decided, "we could make a difference in Kenmore, and we were going to make a difference for kids!" The group returned to the district and proposed to the superintendent and director of staff development that all teachers be trained in the 4-MAT model. The response was an encouraging "go for it!" that set in motion a comprehensive staff development effort.

Turnkey Staff Development

In the summer of 1985, the Madison Six trained a cadre of staff to present 4-MAT workshops in the district. By the end of 1986, all administrators, teachers, and substitute teachers had received awareness training. (Later on, this training began to show results. In 1987, the team added follow-up training in lesson planning, formed a support group to assist teachers in their classrooms, and provided awareness training to all new teachers. In 1988, the district was selected to participate in a nationwide 4-MAT research project to explore ways of helping teachers transfer the theory of inservice training to practice. The results showed that Ken-Ton teachers who participated in both the lesson planning and support group training had, in fact, transferred the skills from the workshops to actual lesson plans and they approached expert status in their knowledge of the model; Miller, 1989.)

The District Climate During Stage 1

No one trusted anyone.

Although there was excitement during the 5 years that made up Stage 1, everything was not perfect. Disorder and lack of trust dominated the district's climate the first year. A board member explains,

> No one trusted anyone. Administrators didn't trust the superintendent, nor did they trust the board to see the change through. ... We didn't have the vaguest idea where we were going. Half the time we didn't have any idea of what we were doing. We were just kind of all fumbling along behind II ID IE IA I!

A union leader recalls that in the beginning, staff adopted a wait-and-see skepticism toward the improvement initiative. Referring to

Project Redesign of years ago, staff reminded one another that they had put together plans before that were, " put . . . in a drawer and nothing happened. This is more of the same. The superintendent will be here 4 years and when he leaves, this will leave."

At the building level, many faculty felt overwhelmed and did not trust the SPTs. To be involved with school improvement was time consuming and it redefined one's work. As one participant expresses it,

> There was just so much happening . . . we were swimming. There were all of these workshops and themes for school improvement. We had so many meetings we didn't know what to do! Besides the facilitator training . . . everybody was being trained in computers!

An administrator acknowledges that early on in some schools, there was tremendous peer pressure on faculty who were involved. Colleagues would ask, "Why are you doing this? Why are you participating?"

There were also ever-increasing expectations. An administrator exclaims, "Each time you did something there were expectations for more, more, more! We didn't get to celebrate one [accomplishment], and somebody wants something else!"

This climate of skepticism, lack of trust, and overload led to a number of challenges that were unique to this early stage of the improvement initiative.

The Challenges of Stage 1

Get on board or . . .

The challenges of working through resistance to the improvement initiative and understanding the role and dynamics of planning teams dominated the beginning stage. Resistance took on many forms from many sources.

Resistance

A teacher suggests that for some, the SIP created an identity crisis: "Here we are, very busy people. We think we're doing our job. We're getting some good results. Then comes the notion of improvement. It made people feel inadequate, saying, 'You mean I've been doing it wrong all these years?' "

Others resisted by waiting it out or by dragging their feet in complying with expectations. For example, "if you attend a 4-MAT workshop, just don't incorporate it in your classroom."

The resistance of the building principals continued. From the beginning, some avoided any involvement with their planning teams. They did not attend facilitator training, choosing instead to assign an assistant principal or program supervisor to accompany a teacher and parent. After all, they were being asked to share both their power and their authority. One observer confesses, "I would have resisted, too, wearing their hat. Someone is kicking me out and asking me to help them do it."

Both soft and hard strategies were used to cope with resistance. The primary approach was to reaffirm the expectation that "it will be done" and then to provide resources and support to do it. A principal explains that, although Helfrich told the principals "we will have school planning teams," many of the principals still dragged their feet. The next step was to present choices and consequences. The superintendent recalls the day he lined the principals up and said:

> Look, your organization's committed to this, the board's committed to this, and I'm committed to this. You've got three choices. One, get on board . . . we'll all be in this together. Two, you can retire. Three, you can "game" me for a while, but sooner or later I'm going to catch on and I'm going to be all over you. So, make a decision!

That laying out of the terrain was critical. A few who were eligible retired. Most, however, got on board either wholeheartedly or reluctantly.

Teams on the Edge of Chaos

They didn't meet often. They didn't do anything risky.

Conflict

One of the earliest conflicts teams had to work through was their role. Understanding the planning process as visionary was not a simple concept. A team facilitator recalls that staff responded by saying, "Don't ask me to think about . . . curriculum 10 years down the line. I can't do that. I don't have a place to park my car!" Until such gripes were addressed, the teams were not productive.

Short-Term Planning

In most schools, the design teams tended to focus on short-term "fix-its"—things about their building that were irritating them. As a result, early projects in many schools dealt with beautification of physical facilities or renovations of common areas, such as cafeterias and meeting rooms. A board member notes, however, that, "it was a good way for people to see results quickly . . . in order to get buy-in."

Role Confusion

Teams had to learn which issues they could handle and which should be handled through the principal's office or other committee structures. To ensure their focus on issues of teaching and learning, some schools formed a separate Committee on Gripes (COG) to deal with day-to-day problems. COGs decided if a task force was needed to explore a problem and recommend a solution.

Inefficient Use of Resources

Some schools tried to avoid conflict by selecting "safe" members of the SPTs. This grew out of a concern that the planning team would be giving the orders and making decisions for the superintendent, the board, and the principals. A principal explains that "we certainly didn't ask people to be involved who might have different points of view. It was very safe. It was very controlled. They didn't meet often. They didn't do anything risky."

A teacher describes such control in terms of the lack of substantive agendas in early team meetings:

> We'd come [to a meeting] and they'd say, "There's not much of an agenda today. What would you like to talk about?" Or there might be a presentation—a statistical rundown of the previous year's achievement test scores or attendance trends over a 5-year period. This would be fascinating for a member

of the community or a parent, but for the majority it was telling us what we already knew. And it was standing still.

Lack of Inclusion

In some buildings, over time, the planning teams became closed organizations and were perceived as cliques. Often that perception was the result of a lack of turnover in membership, that is, "People just stayed on indefinitely." In other cases, it was the result of the perception that teams were dominated by a select group of five or six people chosen by the principal that "did not take on . . . risky projects that impacted curriculum." In still others, "people just did not feel part of the process."

In response to such criticisms, many schools established a 3-year rotation system as well as a volunteer selection process. At the end of each school year, staff indicated by questionnaire or informal note their interest in participating on the planning team or design teams. Until recently, in most schools, those who indicated interest were appointed to the team and, in the interest of balance and so all constituencies would be represented, people thought to be assets to the team were invited to join.

Another strategy, adopted to dispel the perception of the team as an elitist group, was to invite observers to attend meetings. In some schools, the meeting agenda was circulated to all staff, who were asked to respond if they want to attend as observers. Newsletters were circulated following each meeting, minutes were published, and in some instances pyramid group meetings were held to inform the school community of the planning team's work. Unfortunately, the pyramid group concept did not always work. "There was so much skepticism out there that it was difficult for team members to go back and pyramid because a lot of people didn't want to hear it."

Communication Conundrums

Communication was difficult from the beginning and remains a problem. An administrator reports that some people did not know what an SPT was 3 years after the teams were created! Teachers would be asked, "What's your planning team doing?" They'd reply, "We don't have one." A veteran team facilitator remarks that, despite the focus on communication in facilitator training, no matter what facilitators tried—minutes, pyramid groups, feedback requests, sharing as much information as possible—people would still say, "I don't know what they're doing!"

Outcomes of Stage 1

The notion of expectancies became a part of the district's culture.

Despite a rather rocky start, by the end of the first stage, 4 years into the SIP, the district could identify indicators to suggest that the process was beginning to make a difference. By the end of Stage 1, the following had occurred:

- Each of the district's 12 SPTs had identified a vision and planned improvement projects.
- Although early projects were high-visibility, low-risk activities aimed at improving physical facilities, they served to demonstrate success and to build trust in the team and the improvement program.
- As teams grew more comfortable with their visioning role, the focus of plans shifted to include goals and programs for classrooms such as improving classroom discipline, designing curriculum to promote higher-order thinking skills, introducing strategies to deal with emotionally disturbed students, increasing student achievement in basic skills, and promoting teacher involvement in staff development.
- At the district level, providing resources and mechanisms for staff development and empowering staff to train as well as supervise one another were viewed as major trust builders. As one teacher summarizes:

> The Educational Research and Dissemination Project demonstrated that the district supported something the union proposed. Clinical supervision got people into classrooms. Then the 4-MAT model for training— sending people out to be trained [by experts], then coming back to train in the district—those were the major

trust builders that got the school improvement program
going.

A central office administrator recalls that by the fourth year, it was
apparent that the notion of "expectancies had become a part of the
district's culture." For this administrator, that concept is exemplified
in a conversation between two principals following a planning retreat.
Apparently the next new challenge for the district (which they referred
to as IT) had not been made sufficiently clear to them. Expressing frustration, one asked the other, "Well, what is IT this year?" The other
replied, "I don't know! I don't really think I heard what IT was this
year!" That exchange was significant, according to the administrator
who overheard it, as an indication that, "What we had, then, was align-
ing vision—looking to the top for expectations."

To summarize, two major outcomes stand out as representative of
the status of the system at the end of Stage 1: trust in the process was
evolving and an attitude of expecting improvement had been established.

4

Stage 2 (1986–1990)

Getting People to Buy In

In Chapter 3, we showed that what contributed most to launching the school improvement program (SIP) successfully was the district's attention to processes and practices that built trust between staff and senior administration and that increased the capacity of individual schools to make decisions about their futures. Such practices involved the use of team structures and required heavy investment in training teams in the process of visioning and consensus decision making.

During the next stage, the skepticism with which staff reacted to these new practices gave way to acceptance. The years between 1986 and 1990 were exciting as teachers, support staff, parents, and building administrators worked together to make the program theirs. A teacher put it simply when she said, "We had to get 'buy-in.' Most staff were middle aged. These were people who had been here 23 years. We had to find ways to move them." Seeing goals accomplished and expanding the mechanisms for shared decision making were the keys to achieving buy-in. Three important tasks defined the agenda.

The Tasks of Stage 2

Task 1: Support and Recognize New Initiatives

They're not going to pay you to get new desks.

From the beginning, when planning teams approached projects proactively, they received support and funding. Any reasonable request was honored. Even if the project was new or untried, very few requests were denied.

Although the Kenmore-Town of Tonawanda Union (Ken-Ton) Free School District's model was based on empowered planning teams, it was nevertheless initially principal led. The principal's role was to ensure that teams helped determine their school's direction; Superintendent Helfrich held principals accountable for that. One mechanism used, beginning in 1985, was the district's contractual performance-based administrator bonus system. In an early experiment, building administrators received up to $2,000 a year for accomplishments that aligned with the improvement initiative. A principal explains that "it was clear that if you didn't buy in, you either got nothing . . . or you'd get a minimum amount." Another describes the effects of the competitiveness this reward system generated:

> The people who got nothing were really upset. But it put the pressure on. More administrators got aboard and started working at it. So it was infectious. As results started coming in, people who just wanted to renovate their buildings complained that they didn't get the budget they requested. And we said, "Well, you're not doing anything. They're not going to pay you to get new desks."

This practice was eventually replaced with a more broad-based incentive system that we describe in a later section.

Task 2: Empower Many People in Leadership Roles

In some places, teachers are the driving force; in other places, parents are the driving force; and in still others, it's the building principal.

Through planning and design teams, the school improvement process gave teachers and parents an opportunity to make changes in their schools that "didn't have to be the way the principal or superintendent saw things," as one teacher explains. Another describes how the sense of control over one's job motivated many staff to agree to do things they would not normally have agreed to do:

When an administrator comes at you with an idea, and it's going to require a lot more time and energy, and it wasn't your idea, people just dig in their heels and say "No!" But when you are part of the planning process, when it's your idea, you buy in. The amount of time and energy people spent because it was "their idea," was tremendous!

Philosophical quarrels continued among building administrators who championed and those who questioned having teachers and parents in leadership roles. Nevertheless, the district facilitators recognized that to realize the new vision, progress depended on extending the definition of leadership beyond administrators. Such empowerment occurred in a variety of ways:

- The numbers of teachers and parents trained to be planning team facilitators increased each year, as did their participation in administrative retreats.
- Building administrators stepped back from facilitating planning teams to allow teacher-parent facilitators more input. A teacher explains that "in some places teachers are the driving force, in other places it's parents, and in still others it's the building principal."
- The superintendent encouraged broad participation of staff in making presentations about the SIP outside the district. As a principal notes, "If you're out there talking about it positively, you're not going to come back here and bad-mouth it. You become a believer. You're giving your testimony."

Task 3: Refocus and Revitalize School Planning Teams

Basically what they did was meet for lunch.

During the first few years of the program, planning teams in a few schools existed in name only. Although these teams paid lip service to producing the necessary documents, they did not really work at school improvement. In the opinion of one administrator, "basically what they did was meet for lunch." In other schools, teams went through several starts and restarts. They made progress during the first stage,

then plateaued. A teacher's poignant description of one team's transformation after 4 years of floundering, demonstrates the need for
trained facilitators:

> For 4 or 5 years, we didn't seem to have design teams that were
> working. They seemed to exist forever without having a goal.
> Then we went through facilitator training and suddenly . . .
> had a picture of what a school planning team (SPT) could be.
> That is, after doing confidence and trust building skills we
> should really get down to business. Up to this point, it had
> been what we're going to have for lunch at the next meeting
> and where we're going to meet.

What about the design teams? The same teacher continues:

> Design teams should not exist forever whether or not they
> achieve a goal. Everything comes from goal statements set up
> each year by the team. Once we got that set up, people who
> had been highly critical began to participate.

These three tasks were accomplished over a 4-year period through a
sequence of processes and events that continued to require the development of new skills and attitudes and a commitment to new behaviors.

The Chronology of
Stage 2 Processes and Events

Year 5 (1986–1987)

Midcourse corrections.

In the fifth year of the program, the focus shifted to the feedback phase
of the improvement cycle (depicted in Figure 2.1) through a formal
process called *monitoring*. To this point, program evaluation occurred
only informally through status reports made at administrative retreats
and in sessions with district facilitators.

Monitoring

Monitoring is a process for formative evaluation. In the context of school improvement, it refers to gathering data to assess progress toward goals then using the data to make midcourse corrections. The process is used to redirect the plans and processes of planning teams.

Assessing Improvement. Working with | I | D | E | A | facilitators, the district devised its own system of monitoring to measure the improvement process. Planning team facilitators who were designated as monitors attended training sessions on formative and summative evaluation techniques. They learned to construct interview questions; conduct semistructured interviews; and design survey instruments to identify the extent to which something is in place in their schools, how much it is valued, and how it would look in its ideal form.

On a regular basis, yearly or every other year, schools survey or conduct interviews with one of their stakeholder groups. These groups include students, parents, teachers, and support staff. Monitoring teams are "commissioned" by the SPT to develop the survey and interview questions and to set a time line for data collection. A teacher describes the challenge of constructing a survey to assess children's satisfaction with improvements to their building:

> Deciding on questions was difficult because we didn't want it to look like we were evaluating teachers. You know, children may say, "I don't like gym because . . ." then they mention the name of a teacher. So we came up with questions that asked them to agree or disagree with statements such as "I like the color of my locker."

Another teacher provides examples of the setting, the ground rules, and the questioning techniques for interviewing (which typically occurs in groups of 10):

> When I interviewed teachers, substitutes were brought in that day and teachers were relieved of their classroom responsibilities. I'd have the teachers for two periods. You did a warm-up exercise to make people feel comfortable and respect each other. We might say, "If you had the right to establish a school,

what's the one thing you'd be sure that school had?" And then
you went through your questions. The ground rules were very
clear. If you were invited to an interview, you could not mention names, only the situation. What was it you didn't like?
How were you treated? What could we have done differently?
What would you recommend?

Using Data to Refocus Planning Teams. The goal of monitoring is to
assess progress toward goals, therefore its initiation in Ken-Ton contributed to the task of refocusing and revitalizing the planning teams.
In describing a large-scale monitoring project in her school, a principal
discusses the process and how it affects the improvement cycle:

> We surveyed [the school community]—560 students, 500 fami-
> lies, 70 staff members. We surveyed their impressions of the
> projects we were working on and whether they even knew
> about them. That gave us a clue in terms of communication.
> Then . . . in interviews, we asked what they would like to see
> improved or what the school should be like. As a result of that,
> we had our retreat, reformulated our vision, then identified
> some new goals and directions to work on.

Another principal identifies how monitoring contributed to clarifying the role of the planning team and renewed its commitment:

> Once monitoring started, it made things easier because you
> have a sense of what people think is important. Teachers who
> served as interviewers developed a new understanding. Some
> then wanted to be on the planning team. So, it's a feeding
> program. It gets more people involved.

To summarize, by the end of the fifth year of the program, the
strategy of establishing formative evaluation as an integral part of the
team's improvement cycle led to renewing the purpose of the
SPT. During the next 2 years, processes and strategies that intensified
union-district collaboration in expanding opportunities for shared decision making dominated the agenda.

Year 6 (1987–1988)

Unbelievable breakthroughs!

The clinical supervision initiated in Stage 1 not only set the stage for collaboration between the union and the administration but also led to the creation of contractual alternatives to the formal evaluation of tenured teachers. In one option, a team of peers could satisfy the requirement of annual observations of tenured teachers. An administrator describes it as an "unbelievable breakthrough" that set the stage for the district's Mentor Program.

The development of the mentor program contributed to the Stage 2 task of continuing to empower many people in leadership roles. It is seen as a turning point in union-district collaboration, for it was another step, in addition to the process of clinical supervision, toward taking ownership of the profession. Says a union leader, "We share responsibility with the administration in recommending whether a person should continue in employment." We describe below the development of the program to illustrate the persistence and commitment to professionalization required to see it through.

Development of the Mentor Program

In 1985, the New York State Education Department (SED) provided funds for districts to pursue programs to improve the evaluation of tenured teachers. A union leader reflects that in Ken-Ton, evaluation was something no one had been happy with for a long time:

> There wasn't enough evaluation. There wasn't enough criticism. The kind of one-shot "dog and pony show" put on for an administrator . . . didn't work. It didn't help people get better. And the problems we have in the classroom today happened 25 years ago when somebody let somebody get tenure.

Union-District Collaboration. Building on the district's successful experience with clinical supervision, the superintendent and president of the union used the SED grant competition to establish a joint committee to recommend a procedure for evaluating teachers. Within a year, the committee presented a report that the board of education approved in concept in 1985. A member of the committee describes the report as another breakthrough event:

> This was 1985, only the third year we were into any of this stuff. We still hadn't really clarified with some of the schools what was going on with the planning teams, and yet we pulled off getting the concept approved by the board.

But the program was delayed because administrators refused to accept that the governing board consist of a majority of teachers. A union leader reports that "hassles continued for a number of years." The document was eventually accepted in 1987, although other controversial issues arose such as the role of mentors in evaluating non-tenured teachers and intervening with tenured teachers who were experiencing severe instructional difficulties.

Role of the Mentor. The essence of the mentor program was, and still is, to have experienced teachers released from teaching responsibilities to be responsible for the development of newly hired teachers. Mentors are selected from those who are active in clinical supervision and the SIP, as well as those whom administrators and teachers indicate are extremely helpful to other teachers.

The mentor's role is to visit the new teacher's classroom at least once a week for half a day. New teachers receive developmental assistance for 3 years. In the second year, visits decrease to once per month. Mentors provide encouragement and feedback related to classroom management, short- and long-range planning, and instructional design. The mentor is also responsible for submitting evaluations to a policy board.

Governance. A policy board selects mentors and recommends which teachers should be retained based on mentor and building administrator reports. The board comprises nine members, five of whom are appointed by the union and four of whom are appointed by the superintendent. Thus, a majority are teachers. By design, neither the superintendent nor the union president sits on the board. Although by state law final authority rests with the superintendent, in Ken-Ton it was agreed that, "if the superintendent does not take the recommendation of the policy board, he has to go back to the board and explain why."

What is the significance of the long, rather complex process it took to get a seemingly simple concept implemented? The concept of the mentor as evaluator infringed on traditional evaluation procedures and required long debate. Within the parameters set by the state, the role of a mentor is not to make assessments or evaluations. The mentor's purpose is solely to provide support through coaching. The Ken-Ton committee proposed, however, that someone so closely in contact with a new teacher should also decide whether that person "should be in the profession or not."

The issue of mentor intervention with tenured teachers required even more debate. That component was especially significant because, as a member of the committee explains,

> it was introduced by teachers from day 1 in the 1985 meeting. It was not a condition of management that intervention with tenured teachers be included. The teachers themselves brought it up. We didn't talk about putting something together to meet the [conditions] of a grant. We were doing something toward an "ideal" of teacher evaluation.

Including Support Staff in the SIP

In the early years of the SIP, some building teams naturally included support staff. In general, however, these staff were not members of planning teams and therefore did not have a mechanism for contributing to the process. Understandably, their morale suffered. The sense of being taken for granted, in combination with other concerns such as inadequate pay and working conditions, produced a general feeling that support staff were "unprofessional . . . like second class citizens."

Members of the support staff pointed out that "the ratio of teaching and nonteaching staff is almost equal, so if you only have half of your staff involved, you've limited the success of the program." The superintendent agreed.

A planning team was formed of clerical, food service, transportation, and buildings and grounds employees districtwide. Representatives from each of the schools and the central office were included.

From that group, facilitators were identified and trained; within a year, the team had completed its cycle of awareness meetings, held a goal setting retreat, and arrived at its own vision statement: "To develop a positive relationship between staff, students, and community, we all work together to foster trust, communication, self-esteem, and self-improvement."

Once under way, the support staff's planning team became a major contributor to improving district processes. The team conducted a climate survey of all noninstructional employees and discovered that staff "didn't have enough information about where they worked." In response, the team created the district's first employee handbook in 25 years, scripted an orientation video for new employees, and developed an orientation program that introduces new employees to the district's SIP—all of which have been adopted for use by staff districtwide.

The Support Staff Planning Team Spawns Special Teams

The diverse needs of the district led to the formation of more specific planning teams in transportation, food service, and building and grounds.

The Transportation Team. The transportation team, which included bus drivers, attendants, office personnel, and mechanics, reviewed research on bus safety and then produced a safety video that transportation employees use in K-2 classrooms to teach proper loading, unloading, and crossing procedures.

The team also collaborated with high school administrators to develop a uniform discipline code to be followed by all secondary students. In addition, the team developed a mentor program for bus drivers in which experienced bus drivers and attendants work with new employees on defensive driving skills and student management techniques.

A design team pointed out that the district had been purchasing inefficient vehicles and "the people who had to run them didn't have a say" in the purchasing process. Now when vehicles are to be purchased, a team of support personnel writes the specifications.

The Food Service Team. In response to budget constraints that threatened dissolution of the department, a food service planning team collaborated with the administration to turn its department into a self-sustaining operation. When this team began, the operation was $38,000 in the hole. One year later, after much trust building and teamwork, the department was $52,000 in the black.

The Buildings and Grounds Team. Working with the Civil Service Employees Association, this team established a committee to determine district custodial staffing levels. Using a database of information from other districts, as well as accepted formulas and computer systems, a team of engineers, heat technicians, and firefighters collaborated to schedule work and determine budgetary needs. This assured that every building would have sufficient services. Another team assumed responsibility for grounds and facilities, assessing needs and assigning priorities districtwide. Finally, secretaries, tradespeople, and the assistant superintendent of buildings and grounds collaborated to develop a computerized work order system.

Mixed Results. Despite these successes, a support staff member points out there was still a long way to go. The district planning team wanted individual schools to take responsibility to include support staff on their planning teams. This happened in some schools. In others it did not. As a staff member laments:

A lot of people don't value the involvement of support staff. Some still, to this day, don't understand the benefit of having teacher aides involved in inservice training. If a teacher is learning about how to deal with a special education student, why not have the aide learn the same thing?

Nevertheless, involving support staff served the purpose of empowerment. A team facilitator recalls the comments of a bus driver following an inservice training session: "Boy, you know, if a company like Bethlehem Steel, where I worked originally, had done something like this for us, they'd still be in business because I feel like a real person!" The same facilitator proudly recounts that when she makes presentations outside the district, "People don't believe it! Our program is so unique. No one, I have found, is doing what we are doing in staff development."

Year 7 (1988–1989)

We'd like to do this. We think we're good enough!

During the seventh year, three other processes and strategies continued the district's focus on buy-in. Peer coaching, the establishment of a teachers' center, and an award for excellence all helped broaden staff involvement in shared decision making.

Peer Coaching

In 1988–1989, the process of peer coaching was added to the strategies for observing and evaluating teachers. There were, then, three alternatives for tenured teachers: (a) formal evaluation by an administrator, (b) the process of clinical supervision with a team of three or four people, including teachers and administrators, or (c) the process of clinical supervision with a team of peers (teachers only). Nontenured teachers were then, and are now, evaluated through the mentor program.

Integrating Mechanism. After reviewing the research on the implementation of new instructional strategies, a language arts design team recognized that the strategies being introduced through staff development needed to be coordinated. To implement the whole language philosophy, as well as to integrate it with existing strategies such as cooperative learning, higher-order thinking, and 4-MAT, the team recommended the process of peer coaching as a mechanism for integration.

The Ken-Ton Process of Peer Coaching. In the peer coaching model, at the beginning of the school year, a team of two, three, or four peers identifies an area of instruction on which to concentrate, then determines a schedule for observing one another throughout the year. The schedule is documented and submitted to the building principal, who must "accept on faith" that it will be carried out. A principal explains that, in contrast to clinical supervision, peer coaching is a more sophisticated strategy that uses more questioning and data collection techniques. Rather than the observer's subjective view of how the observee is teaching, data are collected on what children are observed to be doing, "but it's data that the observee asked to be collected."

Establishment of a Teachers' Center

In 1987–1988, district administration and union leaders collaborated in the development of a proposal to establish a teacher's center. They were awarded $90,000 by the New York SED. Modeled after the terms of the SED guidelines, the purpose of this center was to administer professional development programs for teaching staff.

A 15-member policy board, made up of a majority (51%) of teachers as well as administrators and university, parent, and nonpublic school representatives, provides governance and quality control by overseeing the direction for programming and establishing criteria for approving credits. All programs, for example, must include an activity, a scholarly product, or a follow-up session. As the director explains, the policy board "is concerned that we're offering workshops with content, where people are not going to sit there passively but are actively involved and come away with something—that professional growth is occurring." Those selected to teach workshops are mostly teachers and administrators in the district. Occasionally, consultants from business, industry, or higher education are brought in. The director describes the center's growth as an evolutionary process:

> The first year, we ran about 13 workshops and we were elated when we got 120 people. In the summer there were more and it just grew. The next thing I knew, we went from registering 120 people a semester to 700 or 800 people.

Such success was due to creative, cutting-edge contracts negotiated in subsequent years between the district and the unions, which tied professional development to incentives. The concept of career credits provided $1,500 to professional staff for completing 15 clock hours of inservice training. This program is discussed in more detail in Year 8 of the process, below.

First New York State School of Excellence

A pivotal event occurred in the seventh year. A Ken-Ton middle school won the district's first New York State School of Excellence Award. Achieving this level of success focused the expectation that all schools in the district aim to be recognized as schools of excellence, with an eye toward attaining national recognition. An administrator explains:

We now have 12 out of 13 schools that have received School of Excellence Awards. I think it's important that it started with one school saying, "Look, we'd like to do this. We think we're good enough. Can you give us substitutes for one day to do the writing?" That's the story. And out of it came the thought or some expectations that the rest of the schools apply. But there was really no master plan. That was a grassroots thing.

The application process for the award is extensive, requiring co-operation and teamwork. It tests the staff's ability to conceptualize what is being done in the school for the benefit of students, parents, and staff. The evaluation process involves a rigorous comparison with similar districts against eight conditions of effective schooling:

1. *Leadership:* How staff and administration accomplish the school's mission.
2. *Teaching environment:* How teaching staff are involved in decision making and how they are evaluated.
3. *Curriculum and instruction:* How the instructional program is adapted to the needs of special populations.
4. *Student environment:* How students influence classroom and school policy.
5. *Parent and community support:* How parents are encouraged to support learning.
6. *Indicators of success:* How student achievement is formally assessed.
7. *Organizational vitality:* How school improvement planning is accomplished.
8. *Special emphases:* How special emphases are reflected in content areas.

Year 8 (1989–1990)

On the cutting edge.

During the final year of Stage 2, two strategies completed the district's 4-year focus on buy-in. They were the concept of cutting-edge labor-management contracts and the expansion of the teacher center to a staff development center.

Cutting-Edge Labor-Management Contracts

In 1989–1990, the teachers union proposed radical restructuring of the salary schedule by incorporating into contract negotiations the concept of rewarding individual professional development efforts. Contracts for administrators, teachers, and nonrepresented staff all contained clauses describing the accrual of career credits. Reducing the horizontal categories of the basic index salary schedule from eight to four (i.e., bachelor's degree, bachelor's plus 15 hours, master's degree, and career credits) and keeping the vertical years-of-service categories the same, the district and unions agreed to provide all professional staff with a fixed stipend on completion of 15 to 20 hours of professional development activity in 1 year. These career credits are not cumulative—they must be earned annually—and the stipend is a dollar amount set by the contract (e.g., $1,500 in the year of the program), not an indexed one. In 1991–1992, after a year of committee work, support staff were included in the agreement. They received a stipend of $750 for completing training hours.

Promoting Skill Diversification. Flexibility and spontaneity in facilitating skill diversification among staff were important considerations. A union leader explains the evolution and intent of the program:

> It's an idea that evolved by consensus between the district and the union partially through formal negotiations and partially through informal discussions. Rather than the "graduate-school green-stamp book" approach to professional development [which paid teachers cumulatively for course work for the rest of their career], the theory behind career credits was continuous renewal in the company of your peers. Uniformity in programs and skill development was not the intent. Rather, it was to provide variety and to discover new themes.

An administrator further explains the meaning of informal discussions as well as the meaning of *cutting edge:*

The contract was completed in 6 hours! Think of four people sitting down for three hours at a working lunch, and doing that twice. That's the contract! The details were worked out in committee. That's cutting edge, as a process.

Mechanism for Recognition. Later, contracts provided additional opportunities for rewards and evaluation. Career Improvement Option II is a unique mechanism for rewarding initiative, effort, and risk taking in a very static and structured environment. It is a process for soliciting ideas, in the form of proposals from individual teaching staff, for improvement projects. On completion of Career Option I (i.e., 15 to 20 hours of professional development credits), staff may submit proposals to a joint union-management committee that awards up to 5 days' pay for carrying out a project that must (a) clearly produce a product, (b) include a process for evaluation, and (c) be shared throughout the district through the staff development center.

In 1991–1992, the district allocated $100,000 for Career Option II funds, and a review board authorized 33 of 55 proposals. For example, a math teacher proposed to analyze SAT results question by question to identify curricular areas and teaching techniques that needed reinforcement. He agreed to share the information with high school staff and to propose strategies for improving the math curriculum. In a conflict mediation experiment, a team of middle school teachers was trained to pilot conflict resolution strategies in their classrooms. In succeeding years, funds for Career Option II increased to $200,000.

These contracts provided career options for every employee. The teacher center thus became the major delivery system for the district's staff development. This required changes in the center's structure.

From Teacher Center to Staff Development Center

In 1990–1991, state funding for the teacher center was discontinued. The district, however, agreed to subsidize the center as a restructured staff development center. All employees, not just teachers, were eligible to enroll in its programs. A teacher aide was appointed assistant director and board membership changed to include support staff. The center director, a former teacher, carries out the policies set by the board. Operations are supported through participant registration fees, union-negotiated state funds directed to the center, and district-subsidized staff salaries.

Operations. The SIP's cycle of monitoring and continuous improvement also guides the operations of the center. Throughout the year, introductory, intermediate, and advanced workshops are offered for all employees. All teachers, administrators, and support staff are surveyed through a written needs assessment to ascertain the number and level of workshops to be offered. To verify results, staff members are randomly chosen to participate in assessment interviews. Based on the results of the assessments, programs are planned for a 3-year cycle.

Assessment. Two types of assessment are used to monitor programs. At the conclusion of each program, Likert-style questionnaires are used to provide immediate feedback from participants on the value of the program and the knowledge and effect of the presenter. Several months following a program, participants receive a questionnaire that asks what they are doing differently on the job. This longer-range assessment is used to determine whether participants have infused what they learned into their everyday teaching, that is, whether there is educational effect on students.

In the view of the center's director two major factors account for its success—empowerment and renewal:

What makes us so successful is it's bottom up. Teachers and support staff perceive us as out there to help them. It's not top down, and they know this. And we are also putting people into the next century as far as technology and teaching strategies.

The Climate During Stage 2

There was enthusiasm, but . . . it was guarded. . . .

The phrase "guarded enthusiasm" is applied by a principal who explains that as more facilitators were trained, as planning teams accomplished goals, as mechanisms for staff development and shared decision making evolved, people saw that the program was becoming a permanent part of their school and gradually became believers:

We were a "graying" faculty. I think this gave us all hope—a new vision that we do have a voice, they do listen. Nothing comes down from the top anymore. And for the first time you had people talking together. Groups were meeting. There was enthusiasm, but at the same time it was "guarded enthusiasm."

This period was a time in which people were learning from one another. An important outcome of the learning was the realization that "it was OK to take a risk. It was OK if it didn't come out quite the way you thought it would. Nobody was criticized." That attitude permeated the district. The atmosphere of risk taking was built into the process by the district facilitators and backed by the board. It insured innovation. SPT facilitators, for example, considered the district facilitators a constant source of support, available "at the whim of a phone call." As one team facilitator notes, "They'd help us work through things so we weren't afraid to try new ideas. Instead of saying 'no,' we would walk through it with them, and they'd say, 'Hey, nobody can fault you for trying!' " A board member describes the permission to take risks as a critical factor in achieving buy-in:

If a design team comes up with an idea and it doesn't work, so what? You go back to the drawing board and try again. And that's when the trust in the entire district started to kick in. Everything started working when people knew they could fail and start again.

This climate of guarded enthusiasm and willingness to risk new initiatives was influenced by a major challenge posed, once again, by planning teams.

The Stage 2 Challenge

A lot of schools were run by dictatorial administrators, which has not changed all that much. It's taken them a long time.

Unlike Stage 1, where the challenge involved the role and composition of planning teams, the challenge in Stage 2 focused on the uneven pace of development and uneven involvement in the school improvement process. The interpretations of a variety of staff lend insight to this multifaceted problem.

- In buildings where the style of the administrator was to include staff in decisions, the improvement process moved quickly. On the other hand, "a lot of schools were run by dictatorial administrators, which has not changed all that much. It's taken them a long time."
- In a contrasting view, Superintendent Helfrich describes the challenge in terms of risk taking:

  > It's taken quite a few years for us to become risk takers, to get some really significant changes made. You can't force somebody to become a risk taker. You can encourage them and support them but you can't force them. So, some of our schools moved ahead more rapidly than others.

- Another observer suggests that, in the beginning, few teams dealt with curricular issues or issues that had to do with fundamental restructuring of "what kids do in schools." It was easy to get consensus about improving the cafeteria for both students and faculty, "but as you get into things more substantial, you have more potential for disagreement."
- A principal points out that such irritants got in the way of people addressing real issues and it was important to work through symbolic battles to get to the deeper ones:

  > When school planning teams first start, very rarely do they go right ahead to curriculum and instruction. They'll start with things that parents, students, or staff members need for their own comfort—like "Is the parking lot big enough?"

Despite disparate levels of involvement across schools, by the end of Stage 2 indicators suggested the program was making a difference in student learning.

Outcomes

The results are striking!

Two major outcomes were finally apparent after 8 years of school improvement efforts. Positive trends were beginning to show in traditional measures of student achievement and community satisfaction. For staff, there was evidence of a new professionalism.

Trends in Student Outcomes and Constituent Satisfaction

By 1990, measures of student progress and achievement showed positive upward trends. For example, the district's Excelsior Award Application presented positive results for the following indicators:

Student Achievement

- *Math:* Sixth grade math scores for the New York State Pupil Evaluation Program rose from 88% above the state reference point in 1982 to 93% in 1988 (to 98% in 1994).
- *Reading:* For the same test in reading, scores changed from 87% above the state reference point in 1982 to 83% in 1988 (to 95% in 1994).
- *Writing:* Fifth grade writing scores increased from 91% above the state reference point in 1982 to 99% in 1988 (to 100% in 1994).
- *Scholarship:* New York State Regents Scholarship recipients rose from 15% of the senior class in 1983 to 23% in 1990.

Graduation and Drop-Out Rates

- *College-bound:* Students going on to higher education increased from 72% in 1982 to 78% in 1988 (to 81% in 1994).
- *Dropouts:* Drop-out rates declined from 3.7% in 1982 to 3.5% in 1988 (to 1.5% in 1993).

Community Satisfaction

- *Budget:* Despite large increases in budgeted dollars for staff development, community support for the budget has remained at 80% favorable since 1987.
- *Bond issues:* Voters consistently have approved bond issues for capital improvements and computer technology since 1987.
- *Continuing education:* Continuing education classes draw between 18,000 and 20,000 adults into the district's school buildings. For a district where 72% of the population do not have children in the schools, this has served as an important vehicle for gaining taxpayer support.

Professionalism Based on Trust

> *. . . treating us as professionals.*

When asked to describe turning points in the evolution of the SIP, without hesitation one of the district facilitators lists six breakthrough processes or events. Staff perceived these same events as evidence that they were finally being treated as professionals.

1. The first year of the improvement program, all teams completed a cycle of meetings and retreats with no abuses of trust— that is, "no one stormed out in protest."
2. Peer clinical supervision was initiated and symbolized a commitment to more autonomy for teachers.
3. The process of monitoring meant "asking tough questions about what we were doing and being prepared to deal with the answers."
4. The restructuring of the teacher center empowered staff to participate in the governance of staff development, and the mentor program was a catalyst to fundamental agreement on the quality of instruction and what ought to be the standard for teachers who to acquire tenure.

5. The Schools of Excellence Award established the belief that all schools warranted such a designation, therefore all were expected to undergo the process of applying for the award as a means of ongoing self-evaluation.
6. The career credits option provided the means to reward people "for what they do in the present, not for what they did years ago."

By 1990, anyone who had not walked into a district building for 4 years would barely recognize it. Teachers had developed confidence in their ability to teach in innovative ways. Schools had established teams. Academic standards were improving. And a range of opportunities for professional development and options for evaluation existed.

5

⊰◈⊱

Stage 3 (1990–1992)

Ownership—Problems and Promise

In Chapter 4, we showed the practices that facilitated teachers and administrators buying in to the school improvement program (SIP). During those years (1986–1990), the focus was on strengthening the efforts of school planning teams (SPTs) to maintain a cycle of continuous improvement and to monitor results regularly. It involved empowering teams and motivating them to take risks in initiating visible and meaningful projects. These efforts were coupled with a focus on communicating priorities through districtwide planning meetings, extending leadership to all levels of staff, and increasing mechanisms for shared decision making and professional development through proactive union-district collaboration.

During Stage 3, more than 8 years into the project, participants were aware of many examples showing that the SIP belonged to the schools. Shared decision making was now standard practice, a part of the system. Hiring employees, awarding tenure, determining building goals—all were done by shared decision making. A union leader comments that it became a way of life, "the way things are done now."

The Tasks of Stage 3

Task 1: Achieve Critical Mass

> *It's so deeply ingrained that it's just the way we do business.*

During this period, improvement through shared decision making was no longer seen as an initiative or something new; rather, it was taken for granted. How did participants know that? What were the signals? Staff at all levels throughout the district could describe a variety of indicators that suggested that a certain critical mass of people had accepted the new methods as standard practice. In his attempt to describe signals of having reached this state of ownership, a district facilitator explains that "it's difficult to quantify the process. At a certain point you get enough people who have power, and the mood becomes, 'You're there'—it's institutionalized! But it's undefined as to what the number is." A board member proposes a metaphor that suggests that a signal of having achieved critical mass is the blending of roles:

> You should not be able to walk into a planning team meeting and say, "You're the principal, and you must be the person who answers the phone." That's the way it is now in many of the buildings in this district.

A building administrator, new to the district, confirms that is indeed, "the way it is": "My first impression was that it was difficult to determine who did what job. I saw people doing things that I would have assumed were administrative responsibilities but who, in fact, were teachers or teacher aides."

An examiner concluding a site visit for the National Schools of Excellence Award reinforces that observation:

> One of the amazing things is that people really don't know what they have here. You could go to a district next door or down state and be in a penal colony. People [in this district] are involved in the process—researching, making decisions, and following through on those decisions—people who, [in another district] normally wouldn't have an inkling as to what was going on.

At the building level, principals describe the process as standard operating procedure in their schools. One principal explains,

> we're [now] doing what a school planning team is supposed to do. In a 2-year cycle, we look at our vision, we look at research to see where we should be heading, we monitor our community to find out what they think is working, then re-

define the vision, establish new goals, and establish new design teams to create programs that will make the vision a reality.

These comments offer at least two telling insights. First, 10 years after the initiation of the SIP, schools were just truly practicing the improvement cycle. This suggests there is a lag time before new structures emerge out of disorder. Second, within the new structures, the complexity of roles increases.

Task 2: Establish a Norm of Continuous Improvement

We have to keep growing.

Although evidence continued to accrue that the school improvement philosophy was in place, staff were also aware there was a long way to go. Several principals explained that "everything hasn't worked. We have a lot of pieces going in different directions which need to be coordinated under one vision. There's still room for continuous improvement."

Teachers also identified continuous improvement as "the name of the game" as they questioned the importance of expecting all schools to be recognized as Schools of Excellence. A union leader explained that staff question the importance of awards not because they are not pleased, but because "they see so much room for correction and improvement." In the opinion of another observer, "the energy that goes into completing an application for an award should be put into revolutionizing instructional programs for kids . . . that's what we ought to be talking about—kids. And these School of Excellence awards are not for kids." An administrator provided an alternate view, noting that from the beginning, two of the core values of the SIP were "benefiting kids and benefiting the adults who deal with those kids. So, what's really wrong with some affirmation to adults and parents in schools?"

As in the first two stages, these tasks (i.e., to achieve a critical mass of staff involved in school improvement activities and to establish a districtwide norm of continuous improvement), were accomplished through a sequence of events and strategies that did not rely on previous processes but in fact continued to require new structures and challenges to the district.

The Chronology of Stage 3 Events and Processes: Years 9 and 10

The strategies and practices that contributed to achieving a sense of ownership during Years 9 and 10 (1990–1992) reflect three major themes. One is continued labor-management contracts with cutting-edge features. A second is expanded opportunities for support staff and stakeholder involvement. The third is using state and national award competitions as a means of self-assessment. In the following sections, we describe each of these themes and the processes associated with it.

Cutting-Edge Contracts

We haven't had to negotiate a contract in the last decade.

Cooperative efforts continued to drive contract negotiations. In 1989, for the first time in the district's history, three union contracts representing teachers, administrators, and support staff were negotiated in an atmosphere of "win-win." A leader in the teachers union explains the process:

> The end of this contract will mark 12 years of no formal negotiations. You get together at lunch. You sit down. You talk about what problems you have, what you can live with, what you want to change, and it's done.

Practices associated with the strategy of continued collaboration provide insight to the meaning of the term *cutting edge*. They include the use of contract language that refers to shared decision making, the decentralization of hiring practices, new administrators aligned with the new philosophy, and acceptance of the intervention component of the mentor program.

Shared Decision Making Contract Language

In 1992, the district took a major step to formalize its commitment to decentralization and to make decentralization standard practice. The state commissioner's New Compact for Learning requires districts to provide evidence of shared decision-making practices and a formal process for team selection. Ken-Ton complied by citing union contract language that describes consensus and site-based management as the district's methods of decision making and identified the SPT as the vehicle through which district goals are accomplished. Although there had been no controversy or grievances over selection by invitation, the Ken-Ton also directly addressed the selection process for planning team members. Selection no longer occurs by invitation, but by election. A union leader explains the courage it took on both sides to risk taking this step:

> We haven't had a consistent structure where members are elected to the teams by their constituency. You get on by volunteering. But whom do volunteers represent and to whom are they responsible? They're part of a group that recommends but they're not speaking for a group. Until now, there hasn't been an impetus from the district leadership, nor from the union leadership, to take a step further. All of us, I think, have been reluctant to leap into the abyss.

In another cutting-edge step, the teachers union and the district worked cooperatively to improve the conditions under which substitute teachers function. The success of the Career Credits Program led to an agreement that substitute teachers receive 4 hours of inservice credits for free through the staff development center.

Decentralized Hiring Practices

An opportunity to look at procedures for hiring new staff members emerged as the district began to cope with the retirement of many teaching and administrative staff. As vacancies occurred, a system that merged collaborative decision making with school control developed.

Interview teams were formed at each building where a vacancy occurred. The teams are composed of three teachers (appointed by the teachers union), three administrators (appointed by the administrators union), two support staff, and two parents. Each team establishes its own criteria, with significant emphasis placed on the interview. An administrator explains how the process works:

> A joint committee of the appropriate union and management representatives reviews all applications and reduces the number to an acceptable interview pool. Interview teams conduct interviews with the pool of 10 or 12 people and submit their first choice to Personnel. There is a [written] agreement that this choice will be honored.

The process applies equally to the selection of administrators, teachers, and support staff.

New Administrators and New Alignments

Along with decentralized hiring practices came new administrators. By 1991–1992, at least four new principals had been hired. All had been instructional leaders and they were fluent in the culture of shared decision making. As they put it, "all we know is shared decision making. We know it! We believe in it! We live it! We breathe it!" They also recognized the complexity and demanding nature of leadership within the philosophy of shared decision making. In their words:

- "There's many layers of expectation. It's not just the running of the school with shared decision making. It's this vision to be the best thing possible!"
- "It's a lot of work getting consensus from people. You can't just 'lay it down.' Our district doesn't operate that way anymore. People would balk at something coming from the top down."
- "You can't push the process . . . So it's going to take a lot of work implementing it."

Intervention for Tenured Teachers

Although the concept had been formally approved in 1987, agreement on implementation procedures for the intervention component of the mentor program was not reached until 1992. In this case (i.e., working with a tenured teacher in instructional difficulty), the mentor's task is to diagnose, to provide feedback and suggestions, and then to withdraw when assistance is no longer needed or useful. There were two optional procedures. In one, experienced mentors would work with tenured teachers who voluntarily agree to be assisted in improving their performance. In the other, building administrators would refer tenured teachers to the program for correction of serious instructional deficiencies.

At the time of our interviews, the intervention process was yet to be tested. Several likely candidates retired. Another case lacked appropriate documentation of the need for improvement. There was also the requirement that candidates must agree to participate. Nevertheless, achieving agreement on procedures was considered a breakthrough. It acknowledged that teachers have a role in assisting tenured members of the profession to improve job performance.

Increased Opportunities for Support Staff and Stakeholder Involvement

> ... from seeing ourselves as individual teachers, each in our
> cell blocks, to seeing ourselves as a total unit with a focus.

Another strategy to achieve ownership was to expand the opportunities for support staff involvement and to strengthen links to the district's business and industry stakeholders. There were also efforts to broaden the district's multicultural program.

Expanded Involvement and Career Credits for Support Staff

The importance of including members of the support staff in the district's improvement program was addressed in Stage 2 with the formation of a districtwide support staff planning team. Such efforts were intensified in Stage 3 through a series of actions that included

- hiring practices that called for including support staff on interview teams;

- facilitator training that was extended to support staff planning teams;
- offering a Career Options I stipend to full- and part-time support staff who completed 15 to 20 hours of inservice training annually; and
- establishing the position of assistant director for the staff development center and filling it by a member of the support staff. The center's policy board was also expanded to include support staff as members.

These actions provided a systematic approach to professional development for support staff, a goal expressed by the assistant director of the staff development center. As she says,

> One third of our support staff are not participating in the center's programs. One reason is, it's threatening for them. They don't see themselves as learners. You've got to get them to take the first step by offering workshops they'll feel comfortable in.

At the individual school level, in addition to sitting on the planning team, support staff were trained as facilitators. Some schools also encouraged support staff to participate in general staff meetings, which, a support staff member claims, has led to a change in terminology:

> The terminology in schools has always been *faculty*, which means teachers. Some of the schools are now saying *staff*, which means everybody. So, anyone who is interested is welcome to attend *staff meetings*.

In addition, the district's annual opening day orientation now includes all staff, districtwide.

Multicultural Efforts

In 1990, the district took steps to address multicultural awareness and affirmative action. A committee of staff and community members created a Statement of Beliefs that the board approved. The statement identifies a set of core values that commit the district to establishing curricula, staff development programs, and intervention strategies to promote acceptance of diversity.

One of the first efforts was the creation of the REACH Program (Respecting Ethnic and Cultural Heritage), which established a systematic process to address multiculturalism throughout the district. Seventy staff members received training to examine cultural sensitivities and to begin programs in their buildings. An administrator explains that in each school implementing the program, a shift in teachers' focus occurred from "seeing ourselves as individual teachers, each in our cell blocks, to seeing ourselves as a total unit with a focus."

Business and Industry Linkages

Close to 75% of the district's residents do not have school-age children. Community outreach, therefore, became a high priority during Stage 3. Through school-business partnerships, a workplace literacy program, and an extensive continuing community education program, linkages with industry and the community were strengthened.

Spearheaded by a member of the board, a partnership with local industry was formed. Instead of looking for financial contributions, the district sought to trade expertise through sharing technology, speakers, and activities. Business representatives joined planning teams, as well as the staff development center's board. In one school, scientists collaborated with the teachers at each grade level in providing science instruction, and the human resources division of a company assisted in reviewing the school's application for the School of Excellence award.

Through a joint venture between General Motors (GM), the State Education Department, and the AFL-CIO, the district helped GM workers obtain high school diplomas. In collaboration with a local hospital, the Community Education Department provided supervisory training for hospital staff and the hospital provided work-study experience as an alternative to the traditional high school experience for students. In cooperation with a number of community agencies, the district facilitated the development of a center that provides a wide variety of services in one location with the goal of helping public assistance clients become self-sufficient.

Competing for Awards

> *It's working because you see tangible results.*

The final theme in the strategies to achieve a sense of ownership relates to the district's emphasis on competing for state and national awards as a means of self-assessment. This strategy resulted in both local and national recognition as an outstanding public learning community. As testament to the success of the school improvement program, by 1990–1991, 9 of 13 schools in the district had been recognized as New York State Schools of Excellence and 2 elementary schools had been designated National Schools of Excellence.

A basic concept of the improvement model is to celebrate success. In addition to representative staff members from each school traveling to Albany or Washington, D.C. to accept their school's award, celebrations honoring the entire school community were held locally. As one teacher remarks, "that's why it's working. You see tangible results."

To satisfy the rigorous assessment required by the Schools of Excellence application, staff and administrators were required to examine programs. In doing this, some wondered if the basic principles of total quality management, common to business and industry, were also valid for schools. A local economic development agency knew "what had been going on in Ken-Ton," and encouraged the district to apply for the New York State Excelsior Award. In September 1991, the superintendent formed a writing team to prepare that formidable application. The assistant superintendent who coordinated the project recalls the process:

> The team had from September to the first week of November— 2 months—to complete the application. They were principals, teachers, staff members, doing their regular job as well as this. People were first assigned [Excelsior] categories but we made switches as it progressed. The final writing team probably condensed 120 pages into 75.

The team provided specific information on more than 35 indicators that were originally designed to recognize quality in business. Although the Excelsior is unique in providing public and education sector awards, the business lexicon challenged the educators. A member of the team comments, "We spent a lot of our time translating. The concept of constituent, for example. What does it really mean?"

The team persisted, and in 1992 Ken-Ton became the first school district to receive the Excelsior Award. In comparing the Schools of Excellence and the Excelsior Awards, an administrator points out their differences:

> The Excelsior is more comprehensive. The School of Excellence award says a school has a lot of projects and a curriculum which is responsive to national priorities. There's involvement and shared decision making. The Excelsior, however, says the district as a whole is committed and is functioning in that way.

The staff's response to these awards and what they symbolize influenced the district's climate during this third critical period of the improvement program.

The Climate During Stage 3

Acceptance and Ownership

Ultimately, it all benefits the education of the children, which is the whole reason we are doing this.

By the end of Stage 3, there was little doubt that school improvement and shared decision making were accepted as standard practice. Both a union leader and a board member notes that the change had been gradual enough so that staff did not even realize how built in the process was—"it's just the way we do business." A member of the support staff suggests that neither the teachers nor support staff unions would "ever buy back into not having a say or being part of decision making." A teacher expresses the feeling of empowerment that accompanied the process of shared decision making: "Other districts don't plan together what's best for kids. This is now the way we do business. As a teacher, I feel empowered. I couldn't work in another district."

A sense of cooperation and ownership emerged from such empowerment. Each planning team set priorities for staff development. Teachers and administrators trained as in-house experts in specific instructional strategies now conducted their own inservice programs. The
inclusion of support staff on planning teams ensured that their needs
and those of their departments were addressed. Two administrators
describe the climate of mutual acceptance that resulted:

> One of the things the staff development program has done for
> the district is bring the staff together in terms of mutual respect
> and admiration. We receive letters and notes about how nice
> it is for workshops to be mixed with anyone from an adminis-
> trator to a bus driver to a custodian.

A teacher explains the resulting sense of teamwork:

> People feel more of a team . . . everyone is trying to improve,
> not only their job and their school, but ultimately . . . the
> education of the children is the whole reason we are doing this.

The Job Is Unfinished

> *I don't think people understand how much*
> *we regard the job to be unfinished.*

Several observers suggest that if any cynicism remains, it relates to the
emphasis on applying for awards. A teacher explains, for example, that
many staff members do not see the Excelsior Award as the outstanding
accomplishment that it is. Rather, they look at it in disbelief and say,
"How did we get this?" Some are not accepting of the award because
they feel they had no direct input into the process that brought it about.
They don't see themselves as contributors:

> The Excelsior Award is a coup but . . . it's kind of removed from
> the faculty. The individual teacher doesn't feel personally con-
> nected to it. It's more important to them when a school gets
> recognized as a School of Excellence . . . because they partici-
> pated in it. The Excelsior award . . . is a recognition of both

management and labor and their willingness to collaborate. I don't think this message has gotten across to everyone.

An administrator acknowledges that those who were involved in writing the Excelsior application were impressed, but is unsure "how much of it filtered all the way down." A union leader summarizes the general feeling about awards:

The Excelsior was anticlimactic. If so many schools hadn't won School of Excellence awards, it would have had more impact. The Excellence award is an equally difficult self-study process. Some faculty leaders are very enthusiastic about the process, very proud of their school and feel the efforts of the faculty deserve this kind of recognition. Others are skeptical about how accurate such an award can be.

The Challenge of Stage 3

Our staff doesn't realize how involved they are.

The major challenge the district faced during this stage was the staff's diverse perceptions of the extent of their involvement in the SIP and the extent to which they believed it created positive change. According to two union leaders,

There are people who don't seem to feel as much ownership, or feel that they're creating change ... A lot of people just don't come in contact with other districts like some of us do, and they don't have any idea that we are light years ahead. There's more than enough opportunities for people to be involved.

A 1992 teacher association survey of attitudes toward the district's collaborative restructuring efforts quantified the extent of this perception gap. The survey asked teachers to rate the extent to which they had meaningful input into the district's shared decision making and improvement activities and the extent to which they were involved in such activities. It also asked them to compare teaching in the district now to what it was like 10 years ago. Although nearly half of the district's teaching staff perceived themselves to be involved in shared decision making, nearly half did not. Less than one third believed improvement had taken place in factors related to student learning during the past 10 years, and less than half perceived the community's commitment to education to have improved. On the other hand, more than half perceived that conditions of teaching had improved. The results certainly confirm the challenge of continuing to achieve critical mass after 10 years of school improvement efforts!

The Outcomes of Stage 3

By the end of Stage 3, 11 years into the school improvement initiative, there were indicators to suggest that, in addition to maintaining positive trends in indicators of student success, both shared decision making and continuous improvement had become accepted practices. Three major outcomes were apparent: Quality results continued; decision making was driven by consensus; and feedback from external reviews such as the Excellence and Excelsior Awards not only confirmed the district's excellence as a learning community but provided suggestions that were immediately incorporated into its agenda for continuous improvement.

Quality Results

A new model of organization.

At the district's annual fall retreat in 1992, the superintendent presented to the school community the following indicators that the 10-year investment in improvement strategies continued to produce quality results:

1. State and national recognition. By 1992, 10 of the district's 13 schools had been named State Schools of Excellence and 4 had received recognition as National Schools of Excellence. The district received the 1992 New York State Governor's Excelsior Award. (Through 1993, it was the only school district to have

achieved it. In the 1993 competition, no award was made in the Education Sector.)

2. The district's media center had been named the best in New York state.
3. Student Pupil Evaluation Program scores were the highest in the district's history.
4. The number of students receiving scholarships had increased.
5. The number of students on honor rolls increased by 36%.

Consensus Is the Norm in Decision Making

No one seems to be in charge or responsible.

At the same retreat, the superintendent proposed a new model of organization that symbolized the district's journey from a traditional hierarchical structure to a decentralized structure in which decision making is driven by consensus.

In Helfrich's model of what he called the Blob Organization, illustrated as Figure 5.1, the district's organizational chart was reconceptualized as a one-dimensional horizontal arrangement in which a series of small, elliptical-shaped "blobs" are encompassed by the larger parameter of board of education policies, priorities, and goals.

At the heart of the system is the teaching-learning act, accomplished through teams and teaching-learning processes. These are supported by all other traditional organizational functions, which relate on a horizontal plane rather than in a hierarchy. For example, the role of central office staff—traditionally the decision makers and power brokers and now called the Central Office Support Team—is one of facilitation, support, and celebration. Similarly, rather than only making and overseeing policy, the Board of Education Support Team assumes a supportive role, serving on consensus-driven planning teams, and has no more authority than other individuals on the team. All other departments are shown in a support role in relation to the Teaching-Learning Team, with two-headed arrows denoting that information, support, and communication flow in both directions.

To the common criticism that "no one seems to be in charge or responsible," the superintendent explained that in a consensus-driven model, "no one is in charge because everyone affected by a decision

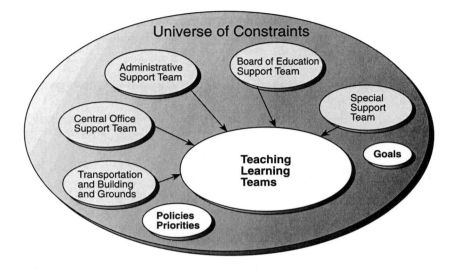

Figure 5.1. The Blob Organization

has had a direct or indirect role in its development, is willing to support it, and will therefore be accountable for results." Failed outcomes or goals are something to be corrected and learned from. Blame, disguised as accountability and defined by clear lines of authority that add layers of individuals who can start or stop a process at any level, is not an essential component of this model.

A member of the support staff describes indicators that confirmed that the model's norm of consensus was indeed operating in the district:

> I can remember in early planning team meetings people were very quiet and did not participate or listen to one another. Now, you don't even have to talk about the process. It just happens. People are willing to get people together to try and solve a problem, to brainstorm, to observe the meeting process and report back. There's a real respect for what everyone has to say as well as acceptance of disagreement, whereas before you couldn't do that.

A third identifiable outcome at the end of Stage 3 was external confirmation of the district's commitment to continuous improvement.

Continuous Improvement

What is world class? We don't know what it means.

In response to the question, "What is it like to be a world-class district?" a board member comments on the district's commitment to continuous improvement:

> What is world class? It may be a label but we don't know what it means. We did not think we had won [the Excelsior Award]. We said, "Even if we don't win, we want to know where we're lacking, where there's weakness." That's what we were all eager to see!

As further testimony to the district's efforts at continuous improvement, at the annual summer retreat in 1993, an |I |D |E |A | consultant presented the following reflective summary of 11 years of progress and accomplishments, attesting to the competencies the district acquired:

1. Eleven years ago, there was a sensitivity to the word *improvement*. Now there is an expectation for change.
2. Eleven years ago, *visioning* was not a word being used by educators. Today, SPTs routinely develop and implement visions.
3. Eleven years ago, *clinical supervision* was a term not widely used, nor did the president of the teachers association and the superintendent of schools use it to give each other feedback.
4. Eleven years ago, the skills to work in groups were being emphasized. Today, in this district, to have building and department facilitators trained in processes such as team building, listening, communication, trust, involvement, and planning is standard practice.
5. Eleven years ago, shared decision making was not a common philosophy. This district understood the need for consistency in using it as a vehicle for systemic change across the district. Shared decision making cannot be used in one school while the rest of the district operates under a totally different philosophy.

6. Eleven years ago, the philosophy that learning is for everyone was not widely adopted. Today, it is acceptable and expected that everyone in the school community is a learner.

The same presenter continued with a series of future challenges facing the district. Posed as four new paradigms to be used in developing a knowledge base for rethinking change, these challenges also suggest a map for understanding the district's path to creating order out of chaos. We explore that map in Chapter 11.

1. Within the uncertainty and chaos in schools, there are important patterns to identify and use.
2. There is a need to move from independence to interdependence.
3. The notion of learning in groups requires a deep, fundamental philosophical shift, not mechanical changes. It is not just five people working together.
4. There is a need to examine what the district has been doing using a different set of criteria, and more rigorous world-class benchmarks and standards.

These challenges set the tone for entering the fourth stage of Ken-Ton's continuing journey to excellence.

6

◇◇◇

Stage 4 (1993 and Beyond)

Focusing on Quality

In Chapter 5, we showed that during the third stage of the school improvement program (SIP), training and teamwork continued, with an emphasis on support staff participation and stake holder involvement. As a means to improve processes, the monitoring of improvement efforts expanded to include the practice of benchmarking through the use of external reviews. In addition, union-district collaboration on compensation and evaluation policies emphasized increased professionalization for the teaching staff.

We also showed that toward the end of Stage 3, the Kenmore-Town of Tonawanda (Ken-Ton) Union Free School District applied for and won the New York State Excelsior Award, an award based on the philosophy of total quality management (TQM). The application process required the district to examine and document what it had been doing using a different set of criteria than is had been using for previous assessments. That self-assessment, as well as examiners' feedback, contributed to an implicit agenda for a new stage with a new set of tasks. This chapter describes the district's direction in terms of quality efforts at the time our investigation ended. As the district completed the first year of this stage, participants identified three major tasks that will shape the future: to renew the focus on student learning; to improve data-gathering mechanisms; and to reconcile district priorities and shared decision making.

Stage 4 Tasks

Task 1: A Renewed Focus on Student Learning

We have reached the end of the envelope in teaching-learning methods.

Members of the district and external observers identified the need for a renewed focus on student learning. To a gathering of the district's leadership at the 1993 summer retreat, the superintendent relayed the message of a site examiner:

> We have reached the end of the envelope in teaching-learning methods. We are pushing the limits of traditional methods. Everything we do now [will lead] only to incremental improvement. We need change in the teaching-learning paradigm.

What did that mean? A building administrator explains that the examiner visited almost every classroom and made this comment: "You have a lot of very good teachers teaching in a very traditional manner." How could that be, after almost 12 years of extensive staff development? Another administrator interprets it as a need to move beyond awareness training:

> We've done a lot of training to make people aware of [teaching strategies such as] . . . cooperative learning. And I can take you into some classrooms where its happening . . . and I can take you to some classes where you might see it once in awhile. People are aware of it. They're trained in it. But they don't feel real secure in it. We've got a ways to go.

Other building administrators corroborate the need for change in instructional methods, suggesting directions for a shift. One proposes that as long as there are standardized tests, "you will have people teaching to the exam, because that's how they're measured. We need to change how we teach so teachers are freed of that." Another suggests the need to change the framework by better understanding

> who our customers are . . . that we are a service industry. That has not been our mentality at all. We have tried to force the

child to fit our mold and our mold is outdated. . . . We need to understand what were getting and where we need to take them.

Task 2: Improve Data-Gathering Mechanisms

> *The bottom line is to improve the quality of learning.*
> *. . . If it doesn't improve, then why are we doing it?*

External observers, teacher leaders, and administrators all recognized a need for sophisticated measures that connect improvement efforts to student performance. One administrator expresses it as a need to find better ways to "come up with cold, hard data about real results." A building administrator explains it as a need to "find ways to gather data which support that something is happening—statistics to show that grades went up 42% over 2 years, for example. But right now we don't have the vehicle or the manpower to do that." A union leader points out the difficulty of making intradistrict comparisons when "we know that our socioeconomic base continues to shift but what we don't know is how much of an impact that has on student performance." The same respondent also notes the problem of identifying data-gathering mechanisms to see if training and staff development have directly affected the classroom:

> We can't . . . sit down and systematically document that be-
> cause these people have taken these courses, these students are
> now performing better. We can't do that . . . We'd have to buy
> the time of a lot of people and even then we wouldn't be sure
> we were doing it well.

Task 3: Reconcile District Priorities and Shared Decision Making

> *How do overall expectations and standards get passed on?*

Another external observer, an Excelsior examiner, poses the following questions in relation to the deployment of standards throughout the district: With all this decentralization and site-based planning, how do overall expectations and standards get passed on? What accountability is there? What up and down communication exists regarding such standards?

For the district, this has led to the realization that it has not yet arrived at a method for reconciling the new decentralized structure with the need for district-level priorities related to curriculum thrusts and standards. An administrator describes several examples:

> It's one thing to talk about whether a school planning team is functioning as well in one school as in another . . . It's another whole matter to discuss whether math or the whole language approach is being taught as well as it should be in a particular school.

Stage 4 Events and Strategies

The district targeted five strategies to accomplish these tasks. To carry out the focus on student learning, it will infuse quality concepts into the classroom, identify exit outcomes linked to districtwide standards, and restructure the way students and teachers are organized in buildings. To improve data-gathering mechanisms, it will incorporate methods of authentic assessment into measures of student progress. And to reconcile district and building priorities, it will expand internal partnerships through continued use of collaborative policy making.

Infuse Quality Concepts into the Classroom

> *After 10 years of the school improvement program*
> *. . . the classroom is probably our weakest point.*

An administrator describes the district's first steps toward the focus on infusing quality into student learning:

> What we're trying to do is get the quality concepts into the classroom so that students understand what it means to do quality work and teachers understand the concept of constituency. We're just at the starting stages. We have quality training workshops every few months and we take the concepts back

to the school planning teams. From there everything is pyramided down.

Training in Quality

The training agenda provides a way of tracking how the concepts cascade to the classroom. At a retreat in September 1992, a pair of consultants trained a group of approximately 75 planning team facilitators, administrators, and community stake holders in the basic concepts of TQM and provided practice in using quality problem-solving tools such as cause-and-effect diagrams, Pareto analysis, histograms, force field analysis, and flow charting.

At a second retreat, in January 1993, participants reported back as to how teams had used the tools at their school sites. One school, for example, used Pareto analysis to analyze the results of a customer satisfaction telephone survey. Two schools used force field analysis—one to identify helping and restraining forces in achieving its annual goals and the second to identify helping and restraining forces in applying cooperative learning strategies in the classroom. A department of the central office used flow charting to understand how to improve communication in the administration building.

At a third retreat, in March 1993, participants learned the processes of benchmarking and partnership management from the manager of the Kodak Corporation's Twenty-First Century Learning Challenge. In addition, through brainstorming, they began the process of defining what quality means for their individual schools.

At a fourth retreat, in May 1993, participants reported the variety of ways quality concepts were beginning to be applied in the classroom. Teachers, for example,

- brainstormed with students about quality work;
- demonstrated and modeled quality work;
- focused attention on measurable outcomes;
- taught students to evaluate their own work for quality;
- considered students as customers, listened to their needs, and asked how to best serve them and parents; and
- used shared decision making by engaging students in planning and classroom management decisions that affect them.

Identify Exit Outcomes

> *We have to stretch kids. If they can achieve*
> *at a certain level, you can expect more.*

The second strategy for implementing the tasks of Stage 4 is directly related to the approach popularly referred to as *outcomes-based education* (OBE). OBE is the basis of the New York State New Compact for Learning, which requires all districts to establish performance, or exit outcomes for graduation. An administrator perceives its application in Ken-Ton as a series of nested results:

> The district should have outcomes. Then each building should have its own outcomes. Each department should have outcomes. Each teacher should have outcomes. And each lesson should have a learning outcome.

The district began the process of identifying exit outcomes in 1992–1993. The experience of one high school provides an example of how the structures of the school improvement process continue to be used as vehicles for change. The administrator who coordinated an outcomes survey explains:

> I surveyed 12 to 15 schools in the country that are already using OBE and listed their outcomes. I picked eight or nine [outcomes] that I kept seeing come up again and again. Then I asked department chairs, the planning team, and the parent-student-teacher association to add any outcomes they were interested in. I wound up with a list of about 20 outcomes, and that became our survey.

In March 1993, a design team distributed 2,500 of these surveys to students, staff, local business, parents, and community residents asking them to identify, from a list of 20, 10 outcomes that the school should strive to achieve. In response to the open-ended statement, " All students will be . . ." 1,535 respondents (61.4%) checked the following outcomes as top choices:

1. proficient readers, writers, and communicators.
2. collaborative workers.
3. quality producers.
4. self-directed learners.
5. complex thinkers, problem solvers, and decision makers.
6. understanding and accepting members of a diverse society and world.
7. skilled users of technology as a tool for learning and work.

The next steps for the team were to provide resources and training for teachers to use the OBE approach. The same administrator describes how this process reinforces quality concepts in the classroom:

> Businesses, higher education, parents, and students are our customers and we have to provide them with skills that are important to them. The business community is telling us, "We want people who can work well in groups." So, a lesson taught in any class, whether it's Spanish or math, should have some sort of outcome to help make the student a better worker within a group. So that, I think, fits right in with total quality management. It's satisfying the customer.

The process of identifying exit outcomes is linked to a third strategy for accomplishing the tasks of Stage 4: incorporating methods of authentic assessment.

Incorporate Methods of Authentic Assessment

> *. . . assessment driving instruction, rather than driving a label on a kid.*

A building administrator describes the change in thinking and instruction required by methods of authentic assessment:

> As long as teachers are held accountable for test scores, the fastest and most efficient way is to lecture. So there needs to be a major change in assessment. . . . A key piece is exit outcomes. Once they are identified and translated into curriculum, the question becomes how do you test it? What are the

tasks that need to happen in classes to asses that students are, for example, cooperative workers? You can't get that on a paper-and-pencil test.

A major component of authentic assessment is the portfolio, in which samples of student work are collected for the purpose of demonstrating or displaying students' progress in understanding, problem solving, and thinking skills. Other examples include the use of running records and read and retell in primary grade reading. An elementary principal points out how the read and retell method is more than assessment by the teacher. It is also a way of involving students, parents, and teachers together in tracking a student's progress in reading:

> The student reads a piece of information, for example, and then writes about it. We look at what has happened to his writing on that piece of information between the beginning and end of the year. There are criteria that every one must meet, such as early reader, emergent reader, and fluent reader. And the writing examples are used for conferencing with parents, as well as the learner. So the assessment isn't just for the teacher.

Another principal explains how the running record method is linked to changes in instruction:

> We're doing . . . what's called a running record on a child. We're actually monitoring and keeping a record of where the child is making mistakes while . . . reading. And what is important is that instruction change so that the child can correct the mistake. That's assessment driving instruction, rather than driving a label on a kid.

These two examples also demonstrate how the use of methods of authentic assessment is an important step in the district's efforts to identify more sophisticated methods of collecting data that link improvement efforts (in this case, changes in instruction) to student performance.

Restructure

> *All students are handled in a team situation, whether*
> *they're super bright or have learning problems.*

A fourth strategy for addressing the tasks of Stage 4 is to restructure the way teachers and students are organized in buildings. In the primary grades, an elementary school was reorganized to a nongraded multiage structure in which a teacher has, for example, eight first graders, eight second graders, and eight third graders all in one classroom. The theory is that younger students will have models to aspire to and older children will have learning reinforced by teaching younger students. In a middle school, an administrator explains that "all students are handled in a team situation regardless of whether they're super bright or have learning problems. All kids take the special subjects with their grade—computers, foreign language, art, music."

The high schools are exploring alternate time arrangements and the number of subjects students take at one time. Long-range goals include reconfiguring schools into smaller, autonomous, highly flexible units operating within a larger context, such as the school-within-a school concept.

The final strategy for accomplishing the tasks of Stage 4 relates directly to the task of reconciling district priorities with decentralization and shared decision making.

Expand Intradistrict Partnerships

> *Systemic change is not simply about schools. It involves*
> *attending to how the components of a system interact.*

An opportunity for improvement identified in the Excelsior examiners' feedback, as well as by members of the district, was communication among the district's components, that is, how district schools benefit from one another's individual experience. A teacher explains that "we realized we don't share enough and now buildings are beginning to send people to visit one another."

Base Groups

Base groups are an example of such sharing and dissemination of successes. Remember the committees on gripes (COGs), formed early in Stage 1 to distinguish problem solving from the visionary function of planning teams? When a task force of a COG makes a recommendation, it makes it through base groups. In 1993, three schools as well as the central office adopted the concept. The entire staff at these four sites formed groups of 4 to 6 people of mixed functions to accept, reject, or modify solutions the task groups recommend. This makes the improvement process all-inclusive rather than merely representative. At staff meetings, employees sit with the other members of their base group, listen to the proposals of task forces, and then turn to their base group to discuss them. Representatives report the group's response to the large group, which attempts to reach consensus. By 1996, most schools in the district had adopted this concept or modified it to suit their own needs.

Collaborative Policy Making

Another problem is the dichotomy between district-level standards and shared decision making or decentralization. A district administrator, for example, raises the question, "How do you get all 13 schools looking together at staff development?"

He answers his own question by pointing out that the staff development center, the mentor program, and new hiring practices are examples of areas where the district is beginning to get "fundamental agreement as to the quality of instruction and what ought to be the standards for teachers."

A source of contention and concern for both the district and the teachers union has been the issue of compensation for participation in shared decision-making activities. In the early stages, teachers did not want to be taken away from their classes, so they received compensation for meeting after school or on weekends—a practice that has been worked out separately in each building. A union leader explains that the contention comes from members who ask, "How come they're doing it and we're not?" or "Are we spending money for people meeting after the school day when we shouldn't be?" He cautions that you have to recognize the fact that different buildings are going to do different things. Buildings will have options . . . but the question is how much leeway is appropriate and how much gets in the way of having a cohesive educational program?

The Challenges of Stage 4

Obstacles to Quality in Student Learning

Many things are working against what we're up to in schools.

The challenges to achieving quality in student learning relate to increasing parental support and decreasing staff resistance to new strategies. The superintendent describes evolving trends in the community that will make it harder for the district to continue to achieve good results:

- "Families are in a state of flux. The number of kids who are abused and the number of kids who get free lunches is higher and higher."
- "We have a lot of parents where the kids run the household while we're trying to develop limits."
- "Parents are more concerned about kids getting bussed to school than they are about learning. They complain because we expect too much of our students."
- "Kids are more violent. We have some fights that I think are very brutal. And authority doesn't mean a thing."

As a result, the superintendent concludes that "we need to do something with parent groups. The more contact we can have with them, the better because we can set some expectations."

Perhaps foreshadowing the possibility that the district is about to enter another cycle of the stages it has just completed, an administrator and a teacher describe the challenge of staff resistance as "getting people to understand, believe in, buy into, and adopt new instructional strategies." This is reminiscent of the very stages the district has just lived through! As an example, they describe two departments struggling with the concepts of tracking and authentic assessment:

> They don't know what to do. They don't know how to do it differently. You can talk all you want about doing away with tracking but they're not trained in having a general-level student and a Regents-level student in the same room and somehow grade them differently. They really don't understand authentic assessment . . . and there's no reason why they should. There have been no specifics.

Echoing the skepticism of Stage 1 are the words of a teacher who says, "Many are intrigued with the possibilities but they are uncertain how much commitment they ought to make to something. How much support will they get from colleagues, from the community?"

Orienting New Members

> *We went through a lot of battles. . . . New people coming in don't know all that took place.*

A second challenge to the district's focus on quality is the issue of staff turnover. This refers to integrating new members of the school community into the district's culture of shared decision making. A union leader notes how, for those accustomed to an adversarial relationship between districts and unions, "the union's role gets a little gray. When the stuff you're promoting says that within your building you get on a team, and you help make some decisions, that's not really adversarial." From the building perspective, an administrator feels that the major challenge for newcomers is understanding the process of shared decision making:

> New people coming in don't realize where we were and where we are today. If you go out and talk to people, they can't tell you where these things came from. If they weren't a part of it, they don't know it happened. The hardest thing has been to

get people to understand the school planning team—how it works and that it does do something.

Change in Leadership

If you don't have leadership that's going to continue to view this as important and keep us moving ahead, there's no way . . .

A final challenge in Stage 4 is posed by the retirement of Superintendent Helfrich. District members expressed diverse perspectives regarding the future of the SIP as they face a change in leadership. In response to the question "Will the process continue after Jack Helfrich retires?" a support staff member replied:

There's no doubt that you need [the superintendent's] and the board's commitment. But I would like to think that if [the superintendent] leaves there's enough energy and support now that it will continue. I think there would be a revolution if it didn't.

A board member supported that view by saying, "The school improvement program is not just his anymore. And he will be the first to tell you it belongs to all of us. That's really what he has instilled in us." Administrators, however were skeptical:

A lot of it has been institutionalized. A lot of the things would go on but if there weren't the leadership there to propagate the philosophy, I'm not so sure. Contractually, you could keep things going, but only for the life of the contract.

A building administrator suggested:

Someone else could come in and because they "control the gold," it could be destroyed very quickly. You have to be willing to put money into staff development . . . So, if you don't have leadership up there that's going to continue to view this as important and continue to keep us moving ahead, there's no way.

This, then was the status of the Ken-Ton District at the end of a journey from decline to excellence. A respected and well-recognized district, as well as a complacent and bureaucratic organization with less-than-challenging expectations for students and professionals, is now one where excellence is expected, power is widely shared, and teaching and learning are the priorities. But the story is incomplete without understanding how participants interpret its success. What were the common threads? What do participants see as most significant? What, for them, were critical factors? Before leaving the journey to present the interpretive aspects of this book, we synthesize and integrate the story by describing five factors participants see as the backbone of the school improvement process.

Synthesis: The Backbone of Success

Visionary Leadership

> *If we have an idea we want to try, they say "Do it!"*
> *How much better can it get than that?*

All participants acknowledged the critical role of vision at all levels of leadership. At the level of the board of education, "Someone needed to propose and support change. A sign that the board valued it was the hiring of Jack Helfrich."

At the level of the superintendent, the key is a superintendent who actively supports visionary leadership, believes it, wants it, nurtures it. Jack Helfrich, "believed in it, and sold it to the board of education. And he brought the board along." At the level of building leadership, principals must "provide the impetus to keep it going because teachers are busy in the classroom. They just can't take off and do things, so you have to support their efforts with administrators' time." Finally, union leadership received much credit for a vision of "establishing a collaborative environment—something which doesn't happen elsewhere."

Comprehensive Staff Development

> *. . . the reason this district is as good as it is.*

Participants emphasize that extending training to parents, teachers, administrators, and support staff was critical to developing site-based expertise. A building administrator succinctly summarizes the importance not only of training but also of providing time to reinforce it:

> I know a lot of schools say they are doing shared decision making but they have not put training into place. You cannot move a district ahead if you're not training. The other thing is time. We have 45 minutes every day before classes begin where we can hold a meeting . . . to go over 4-MAT, outcomes-based education, peer coaching. That time is essential.

Developing Trust Through Ownership

> *Everyone doesn't have to agree.*

Another key factor was the development of trust among all stakeholders. The superintendent modeled this by establishing, "trust . . . with everybody [by] . . .trying to do what he tells you he's going to do." A union leader describes an example of the effectiveness of the strategy:

> The notion of bringing in the union leadership to those first sessions on clinical supervision . . . enabling and encouraging . . . us to jump in on the ground floor . . . was the right thing to do and it worked!

The superintendent explains the importance of involving the board as a major player by fully informing it of the concepts and processes required for implementing the SIP:

> We kept the board involved right along. Most of our board are on planning teams. It gives them a great reason to be very

supportive . . . because they help make those decisions at the building level.

Finally, an external observer paints a compelling picture of the district retreats as an example of the trust and ownership that has evolved:

> There are citizens, support staff, custodians, secretaries, bus drivers, food service people, administrators, teachers. It's a family. You don't see the union on this side and the administrators on that side. They're all together. And everyone has an opportunity to participate in the program. Staff get all the strokes, all the praise. You don't even know Jack Helfrich is there. He's in the back, enjoying himself.

District Support

> *Support is the whole philosophy of the model. We've done so many things that support the basic principles that we accepted.*

Participants describe the critical factor of support in terms of the freedom to fail, to take risks, to experiment, and to find one's own level of involvement, as well as financial resources and external facilitation. A board member points out the freedom that resulted from an internal choice to pursue school improvement, rather than the catalyst being a mandate from outside the district:

> I think it worked so well because we . . . were allowed to fail without mandates . . . I wouldn't want to have to do this . . . under the restrictions that the schools have today. I'm not sure that schools will be allowed to fail.

Other participants note the value of the freedom to experiment and take risks, a tone that was set by the superintendent:

> One of Jack's guiding principles is the fact that you can't stand still . . . gotta constantly be looking for how to do things better, be a risk taker. If you make a mistake, so what? We'll fix it. We want to do things that will make this a better district.

A teacher notes the importance of the freedom to find one's own level of involvement: "I think that what has helped make it successful is that everybody is encouraged . . . to buy in at whatever level they want. Some people just get their feet wet. Others just jump in." Nearly all participants refer in some way to the district's financial support of the change as key to the success of the SIP. A teacher suggests that

> "We don't have the money" is one of the biggest myths that most districts use as a reason to say "No." In this district there is never the sense that "You can't do this because we don't have the money."

An administrator provides perspective on the $250,000 annual cost of the program, which includes substitutes, all staff development costs, subsidizing the staff development center, Career Options I and II, and money for award celebrations:

> Out of $80 million [the district's current budget], that is not much compared to what the private sector would spend on quality improvement and R&D. The truism out of all of this is that . . . you've got to spend money and be flexible in spending it. If you're going to pinch pennies and be hung up on documentation, absolute budget projections, and wanting to know where every cent goes, you aren't going to do anything.

Nearly all participants recognize that school improvement is a process that must be well facilitated. They perceive three types of facilitation to be critical: the support of the external I I I D I E I A I facilitators, the ongoing support of trained internal district-level facilitators, and a critical mass of building-level staff trained as planning team facilitators in human relations, trust, and team building. A building administrator explains the importance of external facilitation, describing the support of I I I D I E I A I as a very important piece:

> We were only able to do this because we had the support of the I I I D I E I A I people. Had we not had that, I don't know where we would have gone, really. They played a very strong role, not just in the beginning, but for years. They came in and introduced the new pieces, whether it was monitoring, clinical supervision, or pyramiding.

In addition to external facilitation, participants acknowledge the need for district-level facilitators. A building principal explains, "They cushioned things. They took information back, so we had a direct line to the superintendent to say, 'This isn't working. People are frustrated.' That's what made it happen."

Finally, comments from the director of the staff development center suggest the importance of a critical mass of staff trained as team facilitators:

> I hear from other directors around the state that their policy board meetings are just brutal—arguments, power struggles, back-biting. The director feels threatened. We have good meetings . . . and I attribute that to the skills of the leaders . . . it's part of their facilitator training.

Long-Term Commitment

This is not something that you can do overnight and without pain.

Participants identify the importance of long-term commitment to achieving school improvement goals. A board member notes that the process evolves

> at conferences. . . . I hear people say, "Oh, we did school improvement last year." And I want to say, "It's not something that you just do!" After all these years, we're still learning. It took us a good 5 years before there was a lot of change. This is not something that you can do overnight and without pain.

Part II

Understanding Ken-Ton's Rise to Excellence

> In the interpretive aspect of criticism, ideas from the social sciences most frequently come into play. These ideas form the conceptual maps that enable the educational critic to account for the events that have occurred and to predict some of their consequences. (Eisner, 1994, p. 229)

The first part of this book gives a detailed description of the transition of the Kenmore-Town of Tonawanda (Ken-Ton) Union Free School District over a 13-year period. This was a transition from decline to growth, from decay to invention, from centralization to decentralization. It's a description of "best practice," that is, a highly detailed account of an award-winning district.

Glickman (1990) and Sizer (1991) caution that truly successful schools cannot be replicated simply by telling other people what the schools are doing. Yet all too often, the writers of best practice make an unstated assumption that the reader will know how to replicate the practice in his or her own district. They omit an essential part of educational criticism, what Eisner (1994) refers to as *the interpretive aspect*.

Eisner (1991) believes that

criticism suffers from its association with negativism. Unfortunately many people think of negative commentary when they hear or read the word *criticism*. But this too is not a necessary or intended meaning. . . . Criticism can be laudatory. It aims to illuminate a situation or object so that it can be seen or appreciated. (p. 7)

The interpretive phase of criticism requires the selection of ideas from the social sciences that help explain the "what" and "how," that reduce the ambiguity of the descriptions so that readers might better be able to avoid the vices and appreciate the virtues as they attempt to apply the ideas.

To be able to apply a variety of theories from the social sciences to the events occurring within schools and classrooms is no simple task. First, one must know the theories that are to be applied. Second, one must be in a position to determine that this particular instance or situation is one for which a particular theory is appropriate. (Eisner, 1994, p. 230)

In this section of the book, we examine the transformation of the Ken-Ton School District from the perspective of five conceptual frameworks. Four of these are drawn from Bolman and Deal's (1991, 1993, 1994) writings on structural, human resource, political, and symbolic frames. A fifth perspective comes from chaos and complexity theory (Gleick, 1987; Stacey, 1992; Waldrop, 1992; Wheatley, 1992). We do not claim to be omniscient about theory, nor are we presumptuous enough to say these are the best theories for understanding and explaining. Rather, our claim is that they provide the reader with a set of theories and interpretations that may make the best practice descriptions of Part I more accessible for practitioner applications.

In Chapter 7, we begin with the framework that is often where practitioners in organizations begin and end their study: the structural frame. Most administrators are familiar with concepts such as line and staff, organizational efficiency, and effectiveness, but they are often naive about variations of structural configurations. In this chapter, we consider the decentralization or downsizing of the central office functions in Ken-Ton and speculate that they resulted in a matrix type of structure.

Chapter 8 highlights the assumed antithesis of structure, the human resources of the organization and how the human aspects of organizations may be enhanced. Chapter 9 deals with a much maligned facet of managing enterprises, the political framework. Here we examine power as a central variable and juxtapose this with the leadership (styles, behaviors) of the superintendent. In Chapter 10, the focus is the "symbolic frame," the cultural aspect of organizations. In particular, we examine a set of organizational rites and ceremonials that are critical for building, sustaining, or transforming a culture supportive of change.

The final framework is examined in Chapter 11, which outlines the work done on understanding chaos. Chaos and complexity are like the alpha and omega of the journey of Ken-Ton (and this book). We began our story with the 13-year journey of a school district that was inundated with the trauma of downsizing and decay, and we conclude by viewing chaos as a "normal state." In doing so, we recognize the discovery of processes that proved useful to the Ken-Ton School District for controlling the complexities of the system and change.

Of course, stories of school districts rarely have endings; they go on in time for what seems like forever. The Ken-Ton School District continues to exist; the schooling and educating of youngsters continues despite the retirements of the superintendent and deputy superintendent, the core leaders who orchestrated the change. But in what condition does the district continue? We end the book with a short epilogue to let readers know what has been happening in Ken-Ton in the years since our formal story and study were concluded.

7

A Structural Perspective for Capitalizing on Chaos

Every organization has a structure, whether through rules and regulations or by hierarchical authority, that holds together the people who work there. Structure is one way of making sense of a system that might otherwise appear random or chaotic. In the case of the Kenmore-Town of Tonawanda (Ken-Ton) Union Free School District, the structure may explain some of the factors that helped the district achieve a vision of "expecting excellence."

Organization structure is frequently viewed as a chart of line and staff relationships (1) that depict a division of tasks or labor and (2) that may be interpreted to suggest the coordination of the work of the organization. Although that picture of structure is useful for understanding the flow of authority relationships, it is insufficient for understanding the nuances of different types of organizations. Mintzberg (1979, 1983) has developed a comprehensive structural framework for describing diverse organization.

Organization Structure and Division of Labor

According to Mintzberg (1989), there are six essential parts to any organization and all have a bearing on its effectiveness as well as being a unique challenge to its leadership. The six parts (depicted in Figure 7.1) are key divisions of labor that take on added significance as an organization grows in size.

In a hypothetical secondary school, one would probably find groups of teachers, clustered in some departmental arrangement, carrying out the normative work of the school. These teachers, together with aides and others performing teaching functions, make up the operating core. In the professional organization, which typifies

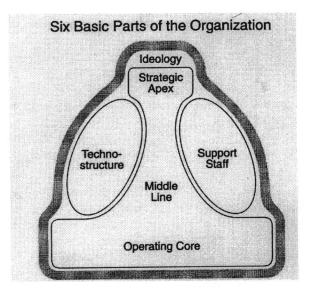

Figure 7.1. Basic Parts of an Organization
SOURCE: From *The Structuring of Organizations* by Mintzberg, © 1979.
Adapted by permission of Prentice-Hall, Inc., Upper Saddle River, NJ.

schools, this part of the organization has a tendency to escape from the controls of the bureaucratic hierarchy, seeking a level of personal, if not collective, autonomy. The teachers want to be left alone to do their professional job of teaching as they see it.

At the top of the school hierarchy is the principal, who relies on a formal or informal cluster of advisers variously called an executive committee, council of chairs, shared decision making team, or kitchen cabinet. Together, they provide both strategic and operational direction for the school and make up the major part of the strategic apex. In a school district, the strategic apex at minimum would include the superintendent and the board of education. These are the school officials who make policy to direct the movement of the organization. Over time, the natural inclination of the strategic apex is to centralize power, to draw more and more control toward the top, and to prevent the other organizational parts from becoming too independent.

Connecting the apex to the operators are the middle-line administrators (department heads) who supervise and evaluate the instructional staff while acting as a conduit for information and resources. In a school district, these middle-line positions form multilayers made up of administrators responsible for articulation and coordination of the diverse school populations, special education teachers, vocational-technical teachers, secondary principals, and the like. Typically in school districts, the last positions in the middle line would be the principals of the various schools, who, in turn, have layers within their schools of assistant principals and department heads.

At each level in the hierarchy, there is a tendency for personnel to seek release from directives coming from above while counting on those below them to comply with their own expectations. Thus, for example, the central office elementary and secondary supervisors work with their departments to articulate the flow of instruction and seek resources for their units—all the while fighting for freedom from restrictive state or district directives so they can do the job as they see fit. In time, these units behave like professional enclaves, paternalistically beneficent but also organizationally myopic. Mintzberg (1989) describes this as the building of mini-fiefdoms of power, a type of "balkanizing" in which there are constant struggles in the competitive market to preserve one's own departmental unit against other collegial robber barons.

Two other parts of Mintzberg's (1989) model come into evidence as a school district demonstrates its concerns for raising revenues, feeding children, coordinating curricula, informing parents, and conforming to the legal mandates of the state. These are functions performed by support staff and a technostructure. In the typical professional organization such as a school district, Mintzberg contends that the technostructure is relatively small in size, mainly containing "analysts" who are responsible for budget preparation, personnel (i.e., human resource management), curriculum coordination, and district planning. Although this sector is only a small part of a professional organization, it has a strong influence on standardizing the work of the district personnel. Offices such as those of business, registrar, personnel, and planning expect all the subunits (especially the core operators, i.e., teachers and aides) to complete district forms in a uniform way and to conform to rules such as submitting requests at particular times.

Another part of an organization of any size are the offices that provide support for the central mission but have little direct effect on the core work, which for schools is the teaching function. These offices are important in their own ways, but the organization could likely exist without them. They include cafeteria services, mailroom or the district's "pony express," custodians, and bus drivers. These offices have little direct influence on operations and thus have little power. They most often voice concerns about wanting to be involved in the decision making affecting the operation of the organization. Rather than seek autonomy, they prefer widescale collaboration that will enable them to use their specialized expertise.

Mintzberg (1989) includes one more element in his personal logo describing structures: ideology. As people in an organization work together, they evolve a set of norms that encourage a unity of mind or togetherness. "It's the way things get done here! It's our way!" For most organizations, such norms are a significant influence on behaviors (for better or for worse). When positive and productive, such norms underscore the values and beliefs that hold the organization together and produce that organization's unique culture. Of course in large districts, with many schools and support units, there may also be different sets of beliefs for each unit, thus spawning unique subcultures.

Organizational Configurations

As organizations grow and develop, over time the basic parts (operating core, midline, etc.) emerge as functional clusters to form different configurations. In his various writings on organizations, Mintzberg (1979, 1983, 1989) describes six of the most common such forms. The bare-boned *simple structure* is how small organizations begin—that is, with a strategic apex (the owner or head) and an operating core (the workers). The corner grocery store operated by parents and children is typical of a simple structure.

If size were a distinguishing factor, at the large end of a continuum would be the *machine bureaucracy.* This is the massive factory, governmental agency, post office, or, more generally, the classic Weberian bureaucracy we have all experienced. It is large and specialized, with formalized procedures and a proliferation of rules. It will probably exist for many years despite efforts to "reinvent government" with all its massive monitoring agencies. All six parts of Mintzberg's logo are found in this configuration; each has a major role in the work of this highly formalized organization.

A third configuration is the *professional bureaucracy,* where operators are professionals (teachers, lawyers, doctors) and professional managers or administrators direct the agency. Typical kinds of this bureaucracy are schools, hospitals, and law firms. "What frequently emerge in the Professional Bureaucracy are parallel administrative hierarchies, one democratic and bottom-up for the professionals, and a second machine bureaucratic and top-down for the support staff" (Mintzberg, 1983, p. 198).

The *divisionalized form of bureaucracy* is characterized as a set of "quasi-autonomous entities coupled together by a central administrative structure" (Mintzberg, 1983, p. 215). In the middle line, the units are generally referred to as divisions and the central administration as headquarters. Often the divisions are either machine bureaucratic units or professional bureaucracies, as with a large university and constituent colleges.

Mintzberg refers to his fifth configuration as an *adhocracy*. These organizations tend to be small, highly flexible groupings of decentralized specialists. Such organizations tend to abhor the classical mechanisms of management and work best when the power resides with the operating professionals. Examples are consultant groups and research teams.

Finally, an organization dominated by its ideological beliefs about the organization and its operations is one Mintzberg labels as *missionary*. "The pure Missionary is built around an inspiring mission—to change society in some way, or to change the organization's own members, or just to provide them with a unique experience—and an accompanying set of beliefs and norms" (Mintzberg, 1983, p. 294). Examples are volunteer organizations, the Israeli kibbutzim, religious sects, and idealistic-driven organizations as Theory Z (Japanese-managed) businesses.

Coordination in the School and School District

An organization is an entity with many elements that are so arranged and connected (i.e., organized) that the various parts pull together to achieve movement toward satisfying a central mission. As organizations grow and develop, it becomes increasingly difficult to focus the efforts of the different elements so that they work together in a purposeful direction.

In a district with as many schools as there were in Ken-Ton in 1968 (28 school buildings), the major organizational configuration would likely be a divisionalized bureaucracy, but it would also take on the characteristics of one or more of the other dominant configurations.

This appeared to be an appropriate description of Ken-Ton. It was a divisionalized bureaucracy and, particularly in the early stages of our case, a mix between a professional organization and a machine bureaucracy. Figure 7.1 resembles the machine bureaucracy in which all six parts have an influence in coordinating personnel and standardizing operations. As the adjective "machine" implies, this configuration raises the repulsive specter of the factory model, in which students enter the system (the school), are processed by production workers (faculty), and exit as educated youngsters ready to become productive citizens of the community.

For the most part, we have come to reject that all-sizes-fit-one model in education, though there are still times when it reoccurs with well-intentioned events (e.g., "standards," if they suggest tolerance levels for product quality, or the "one best way" of teaching that some staff development efforts imply). If we assume that, for the foreseeable future, schools are likely to continue to operate as bureaucracies, then perhaps the most palatable descriptive model would be the professional organization (depicted in Figure 7.2). This model's dominant characteristics are a very large group of relatively autonomous, thinking professionals as the operating core; another large contingent of employees as support staff; a small technostructure; and relatively few levels in the hierarchy that connect the strategic apex to the operating core.

In this model, as Mintzberg (1989) notes, the major mechanism for coordination is achieved by ensuring that the professionals in the operating core possess comparable skills, usually at entry. In schools, for example, this is usually achieved by hiring teachers and administrators who meet the certification requirements of their state. Typically, these requirements have been acquired by completing courses from accredited institutions. Many school districts have made the assumption that schools will have a unified, coordinated thrust if they simply hire "well-qualified" (accredited) professionals who are then turned loose to do as they were trained. During their first 3 years of teaching, teachers are monitored by administrators and socialized to the norms of that school by their colleagues. After that, they receive tenure, giving them a lifetime to display the expertise of their subject matter and teaching prowess.

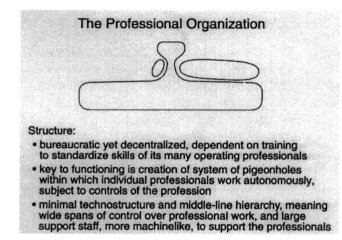

Figure 7.2. The Professional Organization
SOURCE: From *The Structuring of Organizations* by Mintzberg, © 1979, p. 355.
Adapted by permission of Prentice-Hall, Inc., Upper Saddle River, NJ.

Because training occurs prior to hire (from the education programs of colleges and universities), there is little need for a large technostructure in which formalized on-the-job training might occur. Rather, the technostructure uses a personnel department to sift through credentials and to verify the expertise of new hires. From that point on, directors or subject coordinators create a unity of teaching and standardization of outputs through applications of various evaluative devices, directives issued as memoranda, or face-to-face committee meetings. It was not always this way, however.

Some 40 years ago, a great experiment was tried in this country. The National Association of Secondary School Principals and its executive director, J. Lloyd Trump, spearheaded a program of differentiated staffing with large group, small group, and individualized team teaching as an organizing technology (Doremus, 1982). Two schools in Massachusetts were at the forefront in implementing the experiment; for the first few years, they hired new teachers by recruiting graduates of liberal arts programs. They turned down any persons trained at teacher colleges or in typical education programs because they hypothesized that such training would inhibit creative endeavor. Instead, the schools trained their new liberal arts graduates in the technology of teaching necessary for the specialized program unique to these experimental schools. In these schools, the technostructure would have been somewhat larger than in the typical professional bureaucracy. Training on the job through a professional apprenticeship was a way of ensuring standardization of teaching skills; however, that was put to a stop once state certification laws were enacted that specified certification in terms of completion of higher education programs.

Applying the Framework

Because organizations are contextually bound entities serving special groups at special times, they either evolve in their structural configurations or maintain themselves despite the changes (which sometimes means they go the way of the dinosaurs). The latter half of the 20th century has witnessed significant social and economic shifts that have strained the operations of American educational institutions. The Ken-Ton School District typifies an exemplary district that met the challenges and changed to survive and flourish.

At a national level, the 1950s was dominated by curriculum reform with educational leadership coming from eminent figures such as James Conant, president of Harvard University and head of the National Commission on Education. In the 1960s, an emphasis on teacher rights and conditions of employment emerged, bringing to the front unions, personnel management, and collective bargaining. This gave credibility to the view that schools were like industrial enterprises (i.e., factories) and needed to be well managed.

The 1970s saw fiscal crises in one state after another. Education emulated the management strategies of big business with implementation of program evaluation and review techniques, program planning and budgeting systems, and zero-based budgeting. The planning divisions in school districts (elements of the technostructure) grew larger and took on more characteristics of the machine bureaucracy as they standardized the operations of schools to make them more efficient. Concurrently an escalation in enrollments occurred, with commensurate pressure for increases in financial support and a need for more and larger school buildings.

On the heels of this growth in schools, the number of school-age children ready to begin their education declined precipitously. As the shift from growth to decline played itself out, it created pressure to close schools in almost every district. In Ken-Ton, the school population decreased from more than 22,000 students in 1973 to just over 11,000 in 1981, a reduction of 50%. With a loss of that magnitude, the district was forced to close 12 of 28 schools in 1973–1974. That year was the beginning of a prolonged era of chaos.

Many administrators in other school districts met this trauma through crisis management. They used stopgap procedures to preserve budgets, maintain programs, hold down massive transfers, and control disaffection and morale. The prevailing perspective for most schools in America was "management of decline."

Almost 50 years ago, Lewin (1947) considered change as occurring in three stages, with the first being an unfreezing of the system. The chaos of the 1970s and early 1980s was certainly unfreezing organizations of every type, and Ken-Ton was no exception. In contrast to the philosophy of preserving and conserving, Ken-Ton's board, in 1977, decided to incite change by hiring an outsider, the first nondistrict superintendent, to close buildings and lay off staff. For the next 4 years, the atmosphere was one of distrust of administration by teachers and the community. Both the teachers and the building administrators felt similarly threatened. All echoed similar cries: "When will the decline stop—when will I be the next to go?"

In 1981, when the trauma had nearly peaked, Jack Helfrich, another outsider, was hired as superintendent of Ken-Ton. In contrast to the philosophy of preserving and conserving, he chose to view the trauma of social chaos as an opportunity for changing the direction, the focus, and the structure of the system.

At the time Helfrich joined the district, it was structured as a classic divisionalized bureaucracy in which the work of schooling was carried out by relatively autonomous units, tightly controlled by central office supervisors, but otherwise loosely interconnected with minimal interdependencies. As with a swimming, track, or golf team, how one team member performed had relatively little effect on the role or performance of the next. Many teachers spent the major part of the day in their classrooms, unaffected by the actions going on in the other rooms of the building. Much of what was taught was redundant, but who knew about it or seemed to care? Coordination was dependent on the prehire training of personnel, who were then expected to carry out the mission set by a relatively beneficent central office. Most of the teachers received their degrees in education from local colleges or universities, and most were also graduates of the Ken-Ton schools. Thus, both training and values were quite similar across the system.

Coordination (as well as standardization) was achieved through the work of large numbers of subject supervisors housed at the district's central office. We were told that there were so many central office subject supervisors that there were insufficient offices to house them all; instead, desk after desk could be found lining the halls throughout the central office building. The early retirements, the forced layoffs, and the school closings were problems, but they were also opportunities to rejuvenate a seasoned senior staff. In an early meeting with teachers, board members, and administrators, Helfrich announced a number of intraschool transfers of principals—an announcement that was met with heated discussion and considerable dismay.

It was not that principals were lazy or incompetent, but rather that many had become so comfortable in operating their own buildings that they appeared to be more status quo oriented than prone to challenge past practices and strive for new or higher goals. Helfrich believed that something different was needed to inspire and unsettle the system. Building on the unfreezing begun by his predecessor, Helfrich's approach was not simply a reshuffling of personnel; rather, it was a logical set of administrator transfers that he tried to soften with both consideration and support. He knew the system was about to embark on a new process for governance, a process tried at building levels but now to be implemented systemwide. He realized, too, that the journey could not be implemented without considerable training, time, and resources.

Prior to entering the first stage of the school improvement process, the technostructure of Ken-Ton had become swollen with planning units and curricular supervisors so that it more and more resembled a machine bureaucracy. In the professional model (Figure 7.2), the technostructure is typically small, with little or no training function included as part of the organization's structure. How, then, did Helfrich move the organization toward that professional model and provide for the training function? More important, what was the nature of the training?

For most school organizations, any training that does occur is usually focused on the core technology, that is, the direct "improvement of teaching." For a district organization, however, the focal audience is principals of schools, who are concerned with the technologies of managing the organization, improving instruction, and ways to govern the total enterprise.

In Ken-Ton, the vision of the school district was for school-level empowerment, with key decisions being made by those most affected by it. That vision required new processes and procedures for implementation. This was a perspective that predated the reform movement of the 1980s and 1990s. It was an anticipation of what today are mandated school reforms for school governance. That was what the training was about—what to do and how to do it to self-govern. In essence, it was an implementation of the |I|D|E|A| process previously tested in schools but, as applied in Kenmore, implemented at both school and district levels.

Over the next few years, during the first two stages of the process, school personnel received training and a different model of governance and organizational structure started to evolve. Although the district continued to be a professional bureaucracy, it was now beginning to shift to a flatter form. Hierarchical relationships continued to exist, but they were becoming less obtrusive in the year-to-year operation of the schools. The focus was mostly on the development of teaching and learning teams, with other temporary teams surfacing as necessary to support the primary focus. These were the primary considerations of the district during the third stage of its development. The model drawn up to describe the evolving structure became known as the Blob Model of Organization (depicted in Chapter 5).

From the perspective of the organizational structure framework, an analysis of the district's processes and functions makes it apparent that, as the district entered its third stage of the process, it functioned much as a matrix organization. Matrix organizations are characterized by their many temporary (i.e., ad hoc) teams commissioned for special activities, which are dissolved as their purposes are met. A hypothetical depiction of the district as a matrix organization is presented in Figure 7.3.

Although Ken-Ton never described itself as a matrix structure, there are definite indications that it functions as such. Most board members have served on planning teams, the deputy superintendent and other central office administrators are members of multiple school planning teams, and every school draws on support staff, community, and parents to serve on planning and design teams. Because the district appears to function as a matrix, a hybrid model that melds the adhocracy with the professional bureaucracy might be a model that best describes the structure of the district. As we indicated earlier in this chapter, the two bureaucratic forms do similar work but with somewhat different orientations.

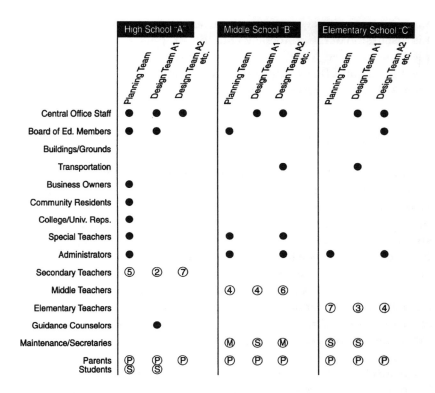

Figure 7.3. Ken-Ton as a Matrix Organization

Faced with a client problem, the Operating Adhocracy engages in creative effort to find a novel solution; the Professional Bureaucracy pigeonholes the problem into a known contingency to which it can apply a standard program. One engages in divergent thinking aimed at innovation; the other, in convergent thinking aimed at perfection. (Mintzberg, 1983, p. 257)

Despite their differences in approach, both operating adhocracies and professional bureaucracies have many elements that make them compatible and strong. Both are typically staffed with specialists (or professionals), both are supportive of democratic governance, and, as we will show in the next chapter, both are capable of enacting a high degree of power sharing while abhorring the mechanistic maneuver-ings of classical machine bureaucracies. Mintzberg (1983) concludes his discussion of the adhocracy with this prophetic statement: "If Simple Structure and Machine Bureaucracy were yesterday's structures, and Professional Bureaucracy and the Divisionalized Form are today's, then Adhocracy is clearly tomorrow's" (p. 275).

Points to Ponder From the Structural Frame

In this chapter, we have examined a framework of organizational structure and used it to trace changes in the Ken-Ton Free School District from a divisionalized, machinelike bureaucracy prior to entering Stage 1 in the school improvement process to its evolutionary structure as a hybrid matrix in Stage 3 of the process. We argue the likelihood that the system approached what Mintzberg (1983) labels an operating adhocracy in the final stages of development. The distinguishing features of an operating adhocracy, with illustrative support from the Ken-Ton School District case, are presented below to provide some ideas that administrators may wish to consider if they choose to move their structures toward this configuration.

> In an Operating Adhocracy, administrators often become functioning members of project (e.g., planning or design) teams with special responsibilities to effect coordination among them; and in that capacity they would be peers rather than supervisors. (p. 259)

The deputy superintendent was often asked to join planning or design teams and he could assist in planning efforts, but our observations indicate his votes or advice carried no more weight than any other team member.

> Support staff play key roles in the Adhocracy so that distinctions between line and staff roles tend to blur. (p. 259)

Almost every planning team ultimately had support staff involved, including custodial and secretarial personnel.

> Unlike the Professional Bureaucracy, the Adhocracy cannot rely on standardization of skills from previous work as a

> mechanism for coordination as that would lead to standard-
> ization rather than innovation. Instead, the Operating Adhoc-
> racy uses the existing knowledge and skills as a base for
> building new skills. (pp. 257-258)

Thus the heavy reliance on the extended training in |I| D|E|A|
process skills, training that must continue if the organization wants to
avoid a natural tendency of such organizations to stabilize and return
to that professional bureaucracy form from which it evolved .

In the next chapter, we continue the analysis of Ken-Ton's process
and look more closely at the extent to which the system was able to
work with the needs of teachers and administrators as it balanced the
trauma of layoffs with the elements of growth and change. How did
the district meet the challenge of creating and operating as an organization in which innovation became the norm, not the exception?

8

People, Professionals, and Perfection

Human Resource Perspective in Achieving Excellence

> *The human resource frame . . . starts from the premise that people's skills, insights, ideas, energy, and commitment are an organization's most critical resource. (Bolman & Deal, 1991, p. 120)*

That professionals at all levels of an organization must be able to work with others, motivate colleagues, and in so doing release their full potential is a *sine qua non* for organizational success. The essence of the human resource frame is not found within a single theory; rather, it rests first on a broad understanding of people and the roles they are required to play within the work environment and second on finding ways to expand and enhance those roles. In this chapter, we consider some of the nuances of the changing roles within the Kenmore-Town of Tonawanda (Ken-Ton) Union Free School District for both the organizational leaders and the followers, focusing in particular on the part that participative management played in the total change effort.

New Roles and the Conflicts Change Creates

A few years ago, a colleague called to our attention a short story by George Orwell (1946) titled "Shooting an Elephant." This autobiographical piece centers on the author's experiences as a member of the police force in Burma. As a European police officer, Orwell knew he was hated by significant numbers of the townspeople. One day he received word that an elephant was on the loose and destroying property. The elephant was tame but had broken loose being in "must," a state of temporary frenzy to which male elephants are periodically prone. Because only the police had weapons in rural Burma, Orwell took a rifle and went to investigate.

When he saw the elephant, he knew that the condition would pass with time or, if the trainer were available, it could be checked and controlled. Unfortunately, the trainer was 12 hours away. At that point, Orwell became aware of the huge crowds of natives that had congregated at the site. He felt their excited adulation; their usual hatred was temporarily transformed into a transient urging of support to kill the elephant. Orwell, however, did not want to shoot the elephant, nor was it a deed he thought necessary to perform at all, for the condition would certainly pass with time. As he looked at the crowd and read their faces, however, he suddenly realized that he would have to shoot the elephant whether he wanted to do it or not. He had no choice!

Orwell (1946) dramatically depicts the power that expectations have on the behaviors of people—for good or bad. The story captures one type of role conflict, the dilemma that members of an organization experience when they sense the expectations of others as incompatible with their own expectations for how to behave. Orwell (as a policeman) knew it is unnecessary to shoot the elephant; he perceived the elephant as "no more dangerous than a cow" (p. 353), yet he also felt the pressure of the emotional support that stemmed from the natives who were anxious to see the kill. His role, at least for the duration of this incident, was as much shaped by the people of the village as it was by the policies of the Imperial Police and his own beliefs and values. This same type of dilemma was experienced by the members of the Ken-Ton organization during the early years of the district's transformation.

In the first year of Helfrich's tenure, the primary force of expectations was from the past, from the traditions of the job: "This is the way we always did it in the past and this is the way we want to do it now." Many of the school administrators had served with at least two previous superintendents who, through the trauma of downsizing, had succeeded in bringing to attention the need to "do things differently." Yet, these administrators had also seen each new district head arrive with a set of expectations diminished in force by how they were conveyed and maintained (in one case, in a negative, harsh, and arbitrary style) or simply dropped with the departure of the superintendent.

Consequently, when Helfrich indicated that the district was embarking on a journey in which schools would become the basic site for change and teachers, community, students, and staff would have equal voices in determining the changes to be made, a few of the school principals shook their heads and thought, "This too shall pass." But this time, the journey was on an express train that would stop at only one station: complete and total change.

As we pointed out in the last chapter, Helfrich continued the efforts of his predecessors to reduce the effects of past school traditions and behaviors by moving some principals to new schools where they could no longer rely on "the old methods" nor on teachers who could be counted on to do things "my way." Using a positive, purposeful, and visionary style, Helfrich provided a process in which all could work together.

The role behaviors of teachers and administrators were to be redefined by the |I|D|E|A| staff development training that ever-increasing numbers of the district were to undergo. To be sure, training in process skills was not new, but to have almost every person in the district involved in the training, many of them at a site away from schools at the expense of the district, was a cost factor that sent a message that this was a change effort to be taken seriously. Even so, administrators in the past and in other districts outlast such approaches by a subtle but effective technique of benign neglect or selective memory. Now, however, they were confronted with teachers, board members, custodians, secretaries, and even parents (serving on school site committees) all exposed to the same intensive training. Thus, a consistent and powerful set of expectations for administrator and teacher roles was being sent from all directions in and across the school organization. These were too potent to avoid or ignore.

Some of the principals found the new system too uncomfortable and chose to retire; others tried to fight the process—"to 'game me' " as Helfrich tells it. But Helfrich assured all the administrators that there was only one game in town, and they could learn it or leave it. In addition, all new appointees to administrative positions acted as supporters who had bought into the one game around. Consequently, teachers found themselves in a vastly different school environment. They had always been expected to teach, and they had done it reasonably well. Now the job was being redefined; they were to be given a say in shaping the total school environment so as to enhance teaching roles and clarify expectations.

The new processes for the district's operations meant that all the staff would need to be resocialized to this new form of organization.

> Organizational socialization differs from professional socialization (Schein, 1986). It teaches a person the knowledge, values, and behaviors required in particular roles within a particular organization. These values and norms may be very different from those the person learned as part of his [sic] professional socialization. (Hart, 1993, p. 11)

Hart's (1993) summary of the literature indicates that there are three key stages of socialization: first, a period of learning and uncertainty; second, a period of gradual adjustment as noticeable changes begin to emerge; and third, the stabilization of the values and behaviors as expected for the particular organization.

As told to us, the uncertainty of the first state was clearly the case for one new appointee to an administrative post in the Ken-Ton School District. This new elementary principal indicates that she felt a pull in two directions from the messages of the superintendent. He emphasized in his administrative meetings that it was important that the board, the community, and the parents see positive results in student outcomes. He emphasized that simply sustaining the achievement levels from past practices was not sufficient; there should be tangible, increased positive results—but he followed that message by indicating that he would also like to see change take place. He seemed to be well aware of the organizational tenet that high-performing organizations constantly seek new ways to do the same things (Vaill, 1978). He wanted to see teachers trying new methods for increased learning. Thus, although he pushed for results, he gave equal emphasis to risk taking.

Being new to the position, the elementary principal was, of course, untenured in her position and therefore she felt extra pressure to perform. Her teachers were relying on her to assist them in shaping or reshaping the school, but she was somewhat uncertain in which direction to take them. As Katz and Kahn (1966) indicate, "all members of a person's role set depend upon his [in this case 'her'] performance in some fashion; they are rewarded by it, judged in terms of it, or require it in order to perform their own tasks." (p. 175)

Consequently, the new principal decided to clarify the problem she was facing; she approached Helfrich. She conveys her dilemma:

> We can refine what we are doing and get some immediate improvement—or we can try out a new program that the teachers have been investigating. The new program may see learning outcomes hold steady or even go down at first—so which path do we take? The sure or the risky?

Without a moment of hesitation, Helfrich responded, "Be a risk taker! I'll support you and go to bat for you knowing you are doing the right thing—even though it may not pan out." In Helfrich's eyes, this principal wanted to be more than a manager of the system; she needed the encouragement and freedom necessary to be an educational leader. Leaders try to do the right thing (taking risks), whereas managers are more concerned about doing things right (sustaining the system).

This principal led her elementary school through the implementation of the new program, received her tenure, and the school was soon thereafter recognized as a National School of Excellence. Some years later, this same principal was asked to take on another elementary school that served a highly diverse population, a school that had rarely demonstrated significant levels of positive achievement with any previous administrator. Within 5 years, that school was also given formal recognition for its achieved excellence. An important aspect of her success can be attributed to her deep commitment to the human resource frame, for, as Bolman and Deal (1992) posit,

> organizations work best when individual needs are met and the organization provides a caring, trusting work environment. Showing concern for others and providing ample opportunities for participation and shared decision-making are two of the ways that organizations enlist people's commitment and involvement at all levels. (pp. 24-25)

The Power of Positive Followers

All too often, we hear about the role of leaders in bringing about change; unfortunately, we often forget the major role that the followers play. Kelley (1992) provides three key observations:

- Leaders contribute on the average no more than 20% to the success of most organizations.
- Followers are critical to the remaining 80%.
- Most people, however impressive their title or salary, spend more time working as followers than as leaders. That is, we spend more time reporting to people rather than having people report to us.

Both Helfrich and the elementary principal mentioned earlier were fortunate to have had followers who bought into the collective and individual visions that were articulated. No matter how strong leaders or managers may be, they are helpless under conditions where teacher suspicion, lack of trust, and insecurity in the job is the rule rather than the exception.

During the first stage of the school improvement change effort, the potential for such behaviors was rampant in the Ken-Ton School District. As we have shown, at the onset of the case description, the district was in the midst of very difficult times. Many of the teaching and administrative staff were under threat of losing jobs or facing involuntary transfers as their seniority rights became negated by massive layoffs. It was a time when a union mentality of contract-management and work-to-rule might have permeated the district and prevented change. Fortunately, only a few teachers and administrators sent such messages; the majority were desperate for change. In fact, a significant element in the district's success was the role the union played in the process.

The union leadership was a positive force in the district and was as supportive of cooperative followership as the new leadership. Both were ready, even anxious, for change. That mutual support was a critical element, because underlying the I I I D I E I A I conception for change was belief in, and training for, participatory democracy. The journey to excellence that the Ken-Ton School District had begun would require significant changes not only in the expanded roles of teachers and administrators, but also in the way parents and community members interacted with the schools.

Participative Management: For Better or for Worse

Although participative management has a long history in both business and education, it has had an uneven record of acceptance and has not demonstrated benefits of productivity (Conway, 1984; Conway & Calzi, 1995/1996, Weiss, 1993). Research on the shared decision making of professionals indicates that not a single study has supported increased productivity with participation. Furthermore, between participation and job satisfaction, a positive relationship has been documented in only one third of the cases investigated. Why this is so is a mystery.

In the Weiss (1993) study, 12 schools with some form of shared decision making were compared with 12 schools without such a formal involvement mechanism. Weiss found that the teachers liked involvement, felt more professional, and appreciated the increased authority and collegiality; however, the involvement did not translate into increased benefits for curriculum, teaching, and student outcomes. Weiss concludes that shared decision making may be a product of reform energy that could better be applied to helping students and student achievement.

As reported in Chapter 5, teachers in the Ken-Ton School District expressed a similar sentiment through their responses to a district conducted survey. At the end of Stage 3 of the school improvement process, nearly half of the district's teaching staff perceived themselves to be involved in shared decision making and perceived conditions of teaching to have improved in the district; however, less than one third believed improvement had taken place in factors related to student learning. Some teachers expressed resentment about taking time from the classroom for such things as training and recognition:

The energy that goes into completing an application for an award should be put into revolutionizing instructional programs for kids . . . that's what we ought to be talking about is kids. And these School of Excellence Awards are not for kids.

A factor that has not received much attention in research studies on participation is the scope of the involvement or, more precisely, the point in the decision making process in which the personnel are involved. In most schools where the concept is mandated (e.g., in New York), the response has been to establish a governance council of teachers, parents, and administrators for each school. These councils have been given limited authority to study problems and recommend decisions (Calzi & Conway, 1995). Wohlstetter (1995) and colleagues at the Center on Educational Governance at the University of Southern California visited 44 schools in 13 districts and interviewed more than 500 people at all levels in the systems. She concludes that all too often a school-based management (SBM) system

> is implemented simply by setting up a council at the school site and giving the council at least some responsibility in the areas of budget, personnel, and curriculum. It is assumed that individual school councils understand their new roles and responsibilities and will take appropriate action to improve school performance. (p. 22)

The tacit assumption that districts seem to make is that having some say through a single council will satisfy teachers and will improve both the quality of the decisions and teacher satisfaction. However,

> if teachers desire a say during the formative stage of problem solving but are only involved at the point of choosing an alternative, then they are not likely to indicate satisfaction with the process despite the fact that they have been involved. (Conway, 1984, p. 20)

Simply establishing a committee for teacher involvement to satisfy some directive or to quiet a voice for reform is not a sufficient response to the problem.

The Calzi and Conway (1995) status report for Western New York coincides with the findings abstracted from the 44 schools reported on by Wohlstetter (1995). Wohlstetter identifies four key items that lead to failure for SBM. A district can expect failure when:

- it assumes that SBM alone is sufficient to bring about an improvement in school performance;
- principals operate from their own agendas as autocrats, despite the implementation of an SBM council;
- districts or schools place all the power in a single council; and
- districts assume that SBM can be implemented with "average levels of commitment and energy" (p. 23).

The Ken-Ton implementation of the I I I D I E I A I model did much to avoid such reasons for failure. Recall that Ken-Ton's vision was and is "expecting excellence," signaling that excellence is neither impossible nor yet achieved. The difference from other districts is how Ken-Ton expects to move toward attaining excellence. Other districts commit resources to developing or refining teaching skills; Ken-Ton has taken a route that suggests that teachers will know best what they might need once they have created their own path and goals. The initial assistance, then, is in creating necessary processes. This does not imply that teachers must be creative or innovative, but rather that they have a set of common processes for making critical decisions about where to go and how to get there. The district took the prudent step of making certain that the skills and techniques necessary for performing those processes were well understood, a decision that was fortuitous in avoiding problems experienced by other districts.

White's (1992) study of three districts identifies difficulties encountered in trying to implement a philosophy of school-based (shared) decision-making. She found that

> teacher participation in school decision making involved a wide array of time-consuming activities, such as meeting to discuss school budget issues, directing and developing new in-service sessions, interviewing applicants for school staff positions, serving on textbook selection committees and curriculum development committees. Teachers lacked specific training in shared decision making, and in school budget, curriculum, and staffing decisions. There was a lack of funding for release time and stipends to participate on councils and committees. (p. 77)

Each of these problems was specifically addressed by starting with a substantial district commitment to I I I D I E I A I training. In the beginning, the district sent personnel to sites as far away as Colorado, where personnel underwent a 5-day intensive training program. That same training regimen continues today, though more often than not it occurs locally rather than off site and it varies in length from 2 to 5 days, followed by a second week for synthesis and reinforcement. The agenda for the initial training included learning about conceptualizations of change, a unified vocabulary around the | I | D | E | A | nine principles of education, skills in process observation so that members of teams could share in providing corrective feedback to their own teams, facilitator skills to guide teams and assure high-level interaction, and the development and implementation of pyramid groups so as to ensure community awareness. The essence of pyramiding (elaborated on in Chapter 10) is an expectation that representatives will initiate and maintain a telephone chain with other people from their particular constituency (e.g., teachers or parents).

We visited many of these school planning teams and could easily identify elements from their training. For example, each meeting would invariably begin with a "WHIP." The acronym stands for a process that "will help improve participation." The first time we experienced this, we were surprised, as it was certainly a different way to begin a formal planning meeting. One example of a WHIP is when a parent stood and challenged the total assemblage to "think of a sound that brings back a childhood memory." The team members talked briefly about bells signaling the ice cream truck, the clang of a trolley, school bells, and the like. After only 2 or 3 minutes, the group was ready to move on to the business of the day. Silly as it sounds, it was effective. For a new member or visitor it was particularly effective. After all, who is going to risk being negative or a thorn in the discussions after that kind of opening?

But even with the best intentions and training, there is still recognition that the system is not perfect. At the first meeting of the school year, a well-established high school planning team asked new members to introduce themselves and for each person to tell why he or she joined the team. One veteran teacher indicated that he was joining the team because he (as well as some other teachers) did not really know what went on at these meetings. "What's all this mumbo-jumbo about? That's why I'm here, to try to find out first hand." The principal welcomed him and acknowledged that, despite all the efforts of the planning team, communicating purposes and processes was still a major problem.

This is first-hand evidence that shared decision making was not, nor was it ever to be considered as, a panacea for school action and change. For many teachers, the permanent committees that have been established in schools act simply as another layer in the school bureaucracy. This is also evidence that implementing new organizational forms is a long, slow, and difficult process. It is a process of change that is never over.

Extending the Human Resource Commitment to Achieving Excellence in Teaching

After a substantial number of the district personnel had completed the process training, and after all administrators had had a second week of intensified work, the district was ready to place greater emphasis on the teaching role. The district's teacher center provided a variety of training opportunities tied to the needs identified at each of the schools. Other training was available directly from district funds through their involvement with the local Board of Cooperative Educational Services.

But training takes time, and for most teachers, time is what they need most to supplement incomes that are typically adequate but not excellent. Recognizing this, the district negotiated a radically restructured, nonindexed salary schedule (described in Chapter 4) that included an incentive plan. For teachers and administrators, this plan provided a $1,500 noncumulative bonus for each year that the staff member accumulated 15 inservice credits. These career credits could be earned by attending university graduate courses, attending teacher center courses, or other study programs. The plan enabled teachers and administrators to upgrade skills while at the same time earn extra dollars; it proved to be very popular.

Another important contribution was the mentor program that was developed to help achieve excellence in the teaching role as well as to socialize new teachers to the expectations of the Ken-Ton district. The program took several years to develop, becoming fully operational in 1989. Guidelines from the New York State Education Department (SED) suggest that districts provide a common planning period or free some time for mentors and novice teachers to meet. Ken-Ton agreed with that goal, but further concluded that the time provided was inadequate to the task. The model is deficient in the long run, for too often more pressing demands deflect good intentions, whereupon the freed periods quickly disappear.

Unlike the approach suggested by the SED, Ken-Ton's mentoring program was designed to use the expertise of experienced teachers in a full-time mentor role for up to 3 years. Each mentor is responsible for as many as 10 new teachers. The mentor spends a minimum of a half day a week in the classroom with each teacher, depending on the teacher's level of development. During that time, the teacher observes, offers tips on teaching and managing behavior, and takes part in hands-on demonstration activities with the students. It's a program that, like the total role expansion for the district described earlier, uses a model of socialization to the profession of teaching as defined by the Ken-Ton district.

Also, unlike the approach suggested by the SED, in Ken-Ton, the mentor's role goes beyond that of coaching to include making assessments and evaluations. Teachers, administrators, and union leaders agree that someone so closely in contact with a new teacher should also recommend whether that person should be in the profession or not.

We observed that the commitment of mentors goes well beyond classroom observations and tips for success. They often contribute personal time beyond the full-time mentoring role. For example, a novice teacher was given an assignment to organize and implement an overnight camping trip. When that teacher's mentor found out that the teacher had never camped in her life, the mentor took it on herself to spend a weekend at the proposed campsite with her so that she would be completely prepared and confident in her teacher-leadership role.

In 1995, there were 6 full-time mentors in the district for approximately 60 new teachers replacing veteran teachers lost because of early retirement incentives. The program is not inexpensive but it has proved extremely beneficial to sustaining a high commitment to change and improvement. According to the district personnel director, the program cost for the 1994-1995 year was about $325,000. That expenditure was partially offset by a negotiated decrease in the starting pay for beginning teachers. The pay remains at the same level for the first 2 years, which offsets the program costs. The program structure and compensation has been accepted by the union because of the long-term personal and professional benefits the program provides.

This program is just one example of changes that occurred at the district level as the total school improvement program unfolded. As more and more of the district's schools gain experiences in the processes for planning and designing, even more human and fiscal needs will be identified, requiring a continued commitment on the part of the system.

Summarizing Some Lessons From This Framework

The human resource frame is not a unified conceptualization, but rests on a belief in the value of expending resources to support the human element in change. It is a recognition of the following:

1. Change entails expanded roles for both professionals and the community.
2. Expanded roles require a commitment to training everyone.
3. Commitment to training is not a one-shot expenditure but rather a long-term process so that the entire district will have access to the processes and the requisite skills.
4. New processes generate more changes, requiring further commitment to training. The career credits and mentoring programs, for example, were the products of teachers, administrators, board members, and union leaders. They resulted in structural changes (new roles and relationships) and demonstrated the district's belief that excellence occurs through well-prepared and well-supported personnel.
5. Change is not an event; it does not begin in organizations. Rather, all organizations must be ever changing as though their existence were a never-ending story.
6. The direction of change is what warrants constant attention. If changing is not toward new ways of achieving excellence, then the organization will stagnate and die—that's the essence of entropy, the natural decay of a system unless there is intervention for growth.

9

The Political Aspects of Change

> *Uncertainty appears as a fundamental problem for complex organizations, and coping with uncertainty, as the essence of the administrative process. Just as complete uncertainty and randomness is the antitheses of purpose and of organization, complete certainty is a figment of the imagination.*
> *(Thompson, 1967, p. 159)*

Despite a shift in thinking about change in which disorder in organizations is no longer viewed as unusual, some semblance of order is desired and is constantly being negotiated, not only by individuals, but also by interest groups that emerge within the organization (Bacharach & Mundell, 1993). That negotiation of order is, in essence, the political frame for analysis. "Different individuals and groups have different objectives and resources, and each attempts to bargain with other members of coalitions to influence goals and the decision-making process" (Bolman & Deal, 1991, p. 190). The concern is with getting things done through and with people. It's about building coalitions, not only of formal groups, but of interest groups as well.

> Interest groups emerge when individuals realize that they have common objectives and may be able to collectively exert enough influence to sway a decision that they could not sway individually. These individuals then form an interest group and collectively devise strategies to pool their resources, exchange them with decision makers for influence, and achieve their common objectives. (Bacharach & Mundell, 1993, p. 430)

145

In the Kenmore-Town of Tonawanda (Ken-Ton) Union Free School District, critical groups were needed to help form and implement the school improvement program (SIP). These included formal groups such as the board of education and collective bargaining units of principals, their assistants, teachers, and aides, as well as informal clusters of those same constituents along with students, parents, community members, and businesses. The involvement of these groups waxed and waned, at times becalmed only to reemerge with new intensity as the district's improvement effort forged ahead.

Although making sense of that political voyage of change is of theoretical interest, it is one step removed from what readers desire. If they are to implement and control change in their own districts, they probably want to know how coalitions are formed and the actions necessary to secure commitment. These concerns suggest that the focus from this perspective should be on the superintendent as a political leader. Bolman and Deal (1994) caution us that the typical conception about leaders that focuses on authority, decisiveness, and command is a leadership trap. It's a misconception that "assumes that leadership is a rational activity, when in reality it is essentially political" (p. 82). We view leadership as "an influence relationship among leaders and followers who intend real changes that reflect their mutual purposes" (Rost, 1993, p 102).

Political Leadership and the Superintendent

In this chapter, we try to make sense of how the superintendent of schools in the Ken-Ton School District obtained the cooperation of the district's diverse groups. The superintendent of a school district is the administrative leader of a large organization that, according to Bolman and Deal (1993), is an arena "in which groups jockey for power, and goals emerge from bargaining and compromise among different interests." (p. 25). Our analysis focuses on the concept of power as a political and social tool of the superintendency; power, says Pfeffer (1994), is the means by which managers influence behaviors and change events.

Understanding Power and Leadership

Nyberg (1990) contends that both formal and informal organizations are ever intertwined with the concept of power: "Where there is organization, there is power also; where there is power, there is also organization. Power is always social because it always involves two or more people who are related formally or informally to a plan" (p. 52). In his extended analyses of the concept, Nyberg clarifies four forms of power that are briefly discussed below.

Form 1: Force

Force is the most discernible form of power, but also the least enduring. The use of actual or threatened harm may illicit immediate support or at least reluctant consent; however, it "is costly and inefficient because unwilling, hostile consent must be maintained under constant surveillance—a situation that requires a large investment of resources" (p. 54).

The superintendent in Ken-Ton was not an advocate of force as a mechanism for change, but neither was he reluctant to make use of threats if they appeared warranted. He would move to this form of power only as a last resort, however. Recall, the church event and follow-up training described in Chapters 2 and 3. Some of the school principals (and some faculty and parents as well) were viewed as foot draggers and reluctant participants and therefore potential disrupters of the endeavor. Superintendent Helfrich confronted the principals with a brief but effective implied threat that they could get on board or chose to retire "but just don't try to 'game me' or you'll lose." In his implied threat, Helfrich sent a clear message that he would be willing to use his authority and his power to get the project under way.

In these early stages of the process, we might argue that the superintendent manifested *contingency-situational leadership* (cf. Hersey & Blanchard, 1977; Hunt, 1984); that is, he was willing and able to shift his own behaviors in relation to the maturity of the group. Where the group was naive and confrontational, he responded with threat; as it opened itself to participating, he shifted to a more interactive set of behaviors.

Form 2: Rhetoric or Storytelling

"A person who is good at using words to turn ideas into images in the minds of listeners and readers is a person of great potential power" (Nyberg, 1990, p. 54). The aim of storytelling is to convince listeners to believe in the plans of the speaker, and through that belief to gain their consent to action. This is a much used power form of politicians, as well as of teachers and scientists. It is also the form in which deception and lying may prevail to gain a point. Whether the storytelling is true or false, fact or fable, positive or negative, in this form of power its purpose is to enlist the cooperation of others for the execution of a plan.

The Ken-Ton superintendent excelled at storytelling or rhetoric. He was persuasive in convincing the board of education to embark on a long and obscure resource-rich experiment. Another key group, the union, was apparently anxious for some kind of change; consequently, Helfrich's story for the Ken-Ton future was welcomed by them. The union was quick to link its organization with the process goals of the district as Helfrich outlined it. Helfrich was also able to convince many administrators and teachers who were "rusting out" in the declining, chaotic district milieu to attend the |I |D |E |A | sessions, despite the jaundiced position that many of them held.

Helfrich's description of a nebulous but positive future for the district was powerfully conveyed and precipitated a change in attitudes among many of the participants. The ability of a leader to "transform" constituents is a current conception of a highly desired form of leadership. Although Burns (1978) first articulated the concept of transformational leadership, it was subsequently adopted by a growing number of leadership scholars who reinterpreted the concept and associated it with charisma. This is certainly understandable, because charismatic leaders seem to possess a power of personality that captivates and changes followers. We, however, follow more closely with the narrow convention formulated by Weber (1947) that delimits the concept of charisma as "a certain quality of an individual personality by virtue of which he is considered extraordinary and treated as endowed with supernatural . . . or at least . . . exceptional powers or qualities" (p. 241). From this perspective, then, the transformational leader's strategies for change emanate not from charisma but from something other than a power of personality.

Wills (1995) sheds some light here: He too contends that there are other than charismatic-type leaders who bring about change. For example, those leaders Wills terms *rhetorical* are able to persuade others to adopt new behaviors by relying for their authority on "forensic" argument (or storytelling). Our observations of the Ken-Ton superintendent indicate that he was more a forensic than a charismatic leader. His prolific reading helped him to stay in touch with new ways of thinking about education. These ideas he subsequently adapted and adopted to become part of his own repertoire for latter argumentation. His style of presentation was intellectual, clear, and convincing, but never bombastic.

To label the superintendent as more reliant on rhetoric than charisma is not to detract from his overall effect as a leader. Rather, it is to underscore that his power for transforming the district and its members came from a set of skills and techniques that can be learned and applied. Bolman and Deal (1994) remind us that formal organizational leaders need not be superhumans with inspired visions to be effective: Counter to prevailing wisdom, leaders are "often the individuals who borrow the ideas of others, package them effectively, and then communicate them powerfully. They are not usually the creative genius. In many ways they are almost always the implementor or constructor" (Conger, 1989).

As we continue to summarize the last two forms of power that Nyberg (1990) has articulated, it will be clear that the superintendent did not rely on any one or two of these forms for his leadership role; rather, all were part of his repertoire, brought to bear as the times were right.

Form 3: Exchange and Bargaining

"In power relations of this sort, consent is bought" (Nyberg, 1990, p. 55). The essence of exchange and bargaining is to reward compliance with some type of economic or psychological reward. The common coinage of this form of power in education is in the assignment to favored schools or classes or to highly desired extra duties in exchange for the cooperative compliance of staff. When the rewards are associated with behaviors such as hard work, high achievement, and extra efforts, then this resembles the more familiar concept of behavioral modification.

The work of the superintendent was closest to transactional leadership as defined by Burns (1978). Burns contends that both the "transformational" and the "transactional" are legitimate forms of leadership, but that many academics have denigrated the latter as being merely managerial or custodial behavior (Enochs, 1981; Rost, 1993). When performing as a transactional leader, says Burns, there is communication with key parties "for the purpose of an exchange of valued things" (p. 19) and such exchanges may be economic, political, or psychological in nature.

Covey (1989) uses the musical *Man of La Mancha* as a potent example of the power of exchange. Don Quixote, the main character, is seen to be a delusional personality who believes he is a knight errant on a mystical quest. One of the extended adventures is Don Quixote's encounter with a barmaid/prostitute who is attractive neither inside nor out. Quixote, however, sees her differently. He bestows a new name on her and tells her she is his Dulcinea. He and his strange ideas are first perceived as outlandish to the barmaid, and she jeers at such a title of respect. But she gradually experiences the power of psychological exchange. The more Quixote treats her as through she were a Dulcinea, the more she begins to alter her behavior. Little by little, she finds herself enjoying the homage he bestows; as a consequence, her actions, her attitudes, and her deep-rooted inadequacies begin to change. She starts to believe in herself. As Covey points out, even at his deathbed Quixote continues his transforming charge to her: "Never forget you're Dulcinea" (p. 300).

The story captures the power of perception; that is, there are benefits in perceiving others to be more than they think they are. It also demonstrates that what some contend to be merely managerial behaviors (i.e., transactional exchanges) may turn out to be the most potent behaviors for transforming another and, in the process, for raising that individual to a higher state of moral conduct.

It was just such behaviors that were used by the Ken-Ton superintendent for changing the district. He encouraged each school to seek and find its own niche; he reinforced attempts at change and rewarded successes—all in an attempt to motivate and transform personnel and their educational practices. But despite his encouragement and optimism, he found it as slow going, as did Don Quixote with his Dulcinea. In Helfrich's words,

> It's taken quite a few years for us to become risk takers, to get some really significant changes made. You can't force somebody to become a risk taker. You can encourage them and support them but you can't force them.

Nevertheless, Helfrich became the number-one cheerleader for what the teachers and administrators were attempting to do, telling them over and over again that they were making significant strides, demonstrating his own belief in them through tangible rewards so that they would eventually believe in themselves. As indicated in

Chapter 5, he urged the principals and teachers to share their successes by applying for state and national recognition despite their reluctance rising from feelings of inadequacy. A union leader notes that many staff questioned the importance of awards, not because they were not pleased to receive them but because they did not believe they were warranted: "They don't . . . respect the awards because they see so much room for correction and improvement."

Yet apply they did, until eventually every school was so recognized, some of them more than once, at more than one level.

Form 4: Trust and Mutual Commitment

The last form of power articulated by Nyberg (1990) is about the power that resonates throughout an organization where people have trust in one another and have consented to a common plan that needs no enforcement. In that condition "time, energy, and attention can be concentrated on the tasks required and not dissipated in surveillance management" (p. 55). Establishing that sense of mutual trust becomes the goal provocateur for this level of commitment.

> At present, there is too little emphasis on learning how to develop trust, to share information, and to work cooperatively on plans that are genuinely and personally held to be mutual by all involved parties. This is where the question of empowerment becomes a useful focus. (Nyberg, 1990, p. 56)

In discussing empowerment, Bolman and Deal (1991) see the central issue for schools to be who has the legitimacy for making decisions that are binding on others. This is just one of a series of concerns that can be raised, particularly if the concept of empowerment is viewed in relation to the research on participative decision making.

Locke and Schweiger (1979) and Dachler and Wilpert (1978) provide a set of dimensions of participative decision making that includes empowerment as one aspect of the total model. The dimensions fall loosely into categories of (1) format (Is the participation mandated or voluntary? Formal or informal? Direct or indirect?); (2) degree (from no participation to complete control and responsibility for the decisions); (3) content (Are the decisions concerned with the organization, personal, or professional work?); and (4) scope (the placement of subordinate involvement in the process, e.g., the stage of problem solving at which participation occurs). All these dimensions need to be considered in establishing the trust level so necessary for mutual cooperation.

Fortunately, these four categories come into play within the |I |D |E |A | process model that the district adapted and implemented. That format, degree, content, and scope were all considered important was, we believe, a critical strength of the program and responsible, in part, for its success.

During this highest form of power building or empowerment, the superintendent manifested what Greenleaf (1977) labels *servant leadership*. Greenleaf developed his perspective of the leader as servant based on his reading of the Hermann Hesse (1956) cultlike classic *Journey to the East*. In Hesse's story, the central figure is Leo, who is first depicted as a servant doing menial chores for a band of men on a mythical journey.

> He [Leo] is a person of extraordinary presence. All goes well until Leo disappears. Then the group falls into disarray and the journey is abandoned. They cannot make it without the servant Leo. The narrator, one of the party, after some years of wandering finds Leo and is taken into the Order that had sponsored the journey. There he discovers that Leo, whom he had known first as servant, was in fact the titular head of the Order, its guiding spirit, a great and noble leader. (Greenleaf, 1977, p. 7)

The essence of Greenleaf's concept is that the servant-leader puts serving as a first priority—a perspective that is significantly different from one that puts the leadership first. Servant-first and leader-first are two extreme types:

> The difference manifests itself in the care taken by the servant-first to make sure that other people's highest priority needs are being served. The best test and difficult to administer, is: Do those served grow as persons: Do they, while being served, become healthier, wiser, freer, more autonomous, more likely themselves to become servants: And, what is the effect on the least privileged in society; will they benefit, or, at least, not be further deprived? (Greenleaf, 1977, pp. 13-14)

The two major thrusts of the servant-first concept were evident in Ken-Ton. The superintendent's vision was to create a system where all the people had leadership skills that they could all apply. It was not a secret society but entirely open. Not only administrators and teacher members of planning committees attended training sessions, all members were asked to attend such training. That meant that parents, custodians, secretaries, and students were invited to learn the skills of group facilitation and decision making; later, they were given opportunities to try out their skills in actual planning or design situations.

As the schools in Ken-Ton became more proficient in developing plans and spawning design groups for schoolwide changes, the superintendent became an advocate for securing the resources and support necessary to implement plans. If a school wanted to try a different schedule that might affect busses, Helfrich would negotiate with the transportation servers to secure the changes needed; when a school designed an alternative to punitive disciplinary rules by renovating a student lounge for high-achieving seniors, he helped the school secure the funds and the space.

In his budget development with the school board, Helfrich successfully argued for funds for innovative practices, staff development, and implementing the proposals of school-developed design teams. He was no longer pulling or pushing for change, but was rather the individual who served the needs of the transformed, change-oriented, system.

Before closing this section, we should mention one additional perspective on power and empowerment that may be helpful for comprehending the success of the |I |D |E |A | process in the Ken-Ton District. Spence (1995) discusses power as a personal force. He contends that by concentrating on the opposing side of a power-power relationship, one tends to diminish if not relinquish one's own power. The power of the opposing side exists in relation to the extent to which the one side grants power or perceives power to be present: "If the other possesses power, but I do not perceive the other's power as effective against me, he has none—none for me" (p. 33).

What follows from this is that empowerment may be better understood as gaining power from the bottom rather than a process of taking power from the top. Teachers were held in high esteem and were viewed as having considerable power at one time, but they lost that when parents and students no longer viewed them as being effective decision makers. So too with administrators.

In Ken-Ton, the | I | D | E | A | "training" was, in part, purportedly to provide a process for making decisions; therefore, it was helping teachers, parents, and others exercise power. We might argue, however, that the training also shaped the perceptions of the parents, staff, teachers, and administrators not only to believe in their own power positions but also to grant (or return) power to those in the school hierarchy. As these participants became exposed to the processes, they learned about accountability and the onerous responsibility that faces educators. In that process, they found their niche for involvement while at the same time returning control to the system.

Some Lessons From the Political Frame

1. Power is important at every stage of the process but not always in the same way.
2. The forms of power that emerge are not equally distributed over the school improvement time period. During the first stage of developing the concept for the effort, the power forms included both force (or threat) and rhetoric (or visioning). In the second stage, buying in, there continued to be storytelling (rhetoric), but now an exchange form of power also emerged. This was often bargaining for tangible resources or personal rewards. During the third stage, psychological exchange became dominant—getting the personnel in the schools to believe in themselves and what they were doing to the point of seeking the recognition they had earned. In the last stage (which is still being redefined with the hiring of a new superintendent), the district came to the ultimate level of trust and mutual commitment. New storytelling occurred, psychological rewards were bestowed, but now more than ever there was an expectation that the school improvement processes would continue and that results would be increasingly more evident in student outcomes.
3. In the change process, leadership is an important element requiring flexibility in style and substance. At times, the superintendent could be described as situational, transforming, transactional, and using servant leadership. Sometimes the styles fell into a sequence, but more often than not they occurred concurrently.

10

The Symbolic Framework

Using Rites and Rituals to Build a Culture of Excellence

> *The symbolic frame assumes that organizations are full of
> questions that cannot be answered, problems that cannot
> be solved, and events that cannot be understood or managed.
> Whenever that is the case, humans will create and use symbols
> to bring meaning out of chaos, clarity out of confusion, and
> predictability out of mystery. (Bolman & Deal, 1991, p. 253)*

As the Kenmore-Town of Tonawanda (Ken-Ton) Union Free School
District implemented the | I | D | E | A | framework, it underwent a
change in the way people acted, a change in their normal modes of
decision making and ultimately in their basic or core beliefs and
values. At the onset of our case description, we saw a district in the
midst of school closings and faculty layoffs.

Just prior to the arrival of Jack Helfrich, one of the Ken-Ton schools
was visited by a group of graduate students in education from the
University at Buffalo. The students' charge was to ascertain the organizational health of the school by looking (and only looking) at the
school environment—as though they were the proverbial aliens from
outer space trying to understand a foreign culture. When they returned
to the university to share their observations, they commented on a
strange feeling of fatalism that seemed to permeate the school. They
maintained that the school seemed to be withering away. There were
no pictures on the walls; the halls were dark, clean, but empty of school
life. The teachers spent most of their time in the classrooms, rarely

interacting with one another, even during lunch breaks. What was going on here?

Later in the term, we learned that this school was in a difficult neighborhood and was not often requested as an assignment by teachers with seniority. Consequently, when openings occurred in that school, the lowest-ranking teachers in the district were placed there— an assignment that carried with it the message that these teachers were next on the teaching ladder to be let go. The school symbolized to many that their teaching time in that district was limited. It was not surprising, therefore, to find faculty and administrators as much (or maybe more) concerned about their own security than about educating youngsters.

Nor was the central office immune. It too was crowded with supervisors who were gradually being moved back into schools or not being replaced when they retired. The top levels of the central office were viewed as unfeeling bureaucrats who were brought in to cut budgets, schools, and people. This was the climate at the time of the change in superintendents. But the change did not bring instant relief—the reductions in force continued.

This climate of pessimism, with its accompanying expectations of failure and apparent feelings of isolation, did not persist for long. As the school improvement process got under way and as it became embedded in the district, it fostered a different set of group norms and values and, consequently, gave birth to a new set of traditions in the district. To understand these changes better, we turn to the language of anthropology and consider the process as changing the organizational culture of the district.

The concept of organizational culture has been popularized (and distorted) over the past decade. Definitions abound—the worst of them equating culture with climate. Rather than underscore the confusion by citing the many variations, we define *organizational culture* as

> the pattern of basic assumptions that a given group has invented, discovered, or developed in learning to cope with its problems of external adaptation and internal integration, and that have worked well enough to be considered valid, and, therefore, to be taught to new members as the correct way to perceive, think, and feel in relation to those problems. (Schein, 1984, p. 3)

This pattern of expectations and beliefs (or invented basic assumptions) produces the norms of the system that, in turn, shape the behaviors of the individuals and groups in that organization. *Climate* is a measure of whether or not expectations are being met; *culture* is a description of the expectations themselves. "What climate really measures then, is the fit between the culture and the individual values of the employees" (Schwartz & Davis, 1981, p. 3).

The question that guides this chapter is, how did the new set of expectations come to be? Saying it another way, How did the new culture—symbolized by the phrase, "expecting excellence,"—replace the culture we first depicted as "expecting doom and gloom?" It would be foolish to say that the superintendent set out to make a deliberate change in the organization's culture. Rather, it is our belief that he had an agenda, built on valid experiences, coupled with some good sense, that he followed faithfully. But we need to know why his intuitive foresight was successful.

Changing Culture Through Rites and Ceremonials

As Trice and Beyer (1984) note, there are generally two major ways cultures in organizations change: through the behaviors of the leaders and through general socialization processes. The leader is a symbol for followers to emulate—thus, a change in superintendents may be an important initiating factor. The socialization process in organizations is an accumulation of experiences that, in Ken-Ton, was significantly influenced through the training and staff development programs. Important as these explanations are, we feel, as do Trice and Beyer, that they are insufficient. Perhaps we can better understand the culture change if we look more closely at the socialization experiences as rites (such as rites of passage) that were organized and planned to influence changes in the basic assumptions of the district members.

Van Gennep (1906/1960) states that "the life of an individual in any society is a series of passages from one age to another and from one occupation to another" (pp. 2-3). He indicates that the special category we know as rites of passage (or transition) include rites of separation and rites of incorporation as well.

Trice and Beyer (1984) extend the work of cultural analysis and apply it to both individuals and groups in organizations. They define rites as formal, elaborate, dramatic but public activities that express selected organizational beliefs or values. Trice and Beyer's framework includes six categories of rites, the first three applicable to individuals and the last three applicable to groups in organizations. These are briefly presented and discussed below, with particular emphasis given, when appropriate, to their explanatory applicability for the Ken-Ton school improvement process.

Rites With a Primary Effect on Individuals

Some rites have a primary effect on the person and at the same time a secondary effect to reinforce or communicate the values and beliefs of the organization. They are important indicators of an organization's culture.

Rites of Passage

Rites of passage are the ceremonies that separate a person from one status level and help move that person to a higher one. Examples in education would be granting of tenure or promotion from within, as when moving from teacher to administrator (Conway, 1990). At the start of the school improvement process, Ken-Ton was no more elaborate in advancing the status of personnel than other districts; however, after the improvement program was well underway, it modified its tenuring process by adding the requirement that teachers have close contact with a probationary teacher. The probationary teacher's mentor would make a positive (or negative) recommendation to the mentor board that, in turn, after synthesizing knowledge from teacher colleagues, would make a recommendation to the board to grant or withhold tenure (see Chapter 4). This elaborate system sent various messages to the membership that supported their professional roles as teachers and reinforced trust in their judgments.

The district sent another symbolic message through the system in making appointments of new principals from within the district so as to maintain program continuity—a shift in district policy that clearly demonstrated a continuing commitment to the total school improvement endeavor.

Rites of Enhancement

Deal and Peterson (1990), Bolman and Deal (1991), and others suggest that a starting process for sizing up an organization's culture is to identify, listen to, and interpret the stories and special events from past heroes and heroines. *Enhancement rites* are an important process by which people are granted formal "hero" status. These are acts of formal recognition that not only make high-performing individuals feel good about themselves but also increase their social influence in the system (hence the hero status).

Typically, these rites are of the nature of "teacher of the year" bestowed by the parent-teacher association. Such recognition, however, is short lived and often perceived as a sham: "Whose turn is it this year?" (Conway, 1990). Even when the honor is deserved, a few days after the ceremony the district personnel and community are often hard put to recall either the recipient or the reasons for the recognition.

Student scholars and athletes in a single school often receive acclaim with a posted picture in their school. That's difficult to emulate for teachers or administrators because rarely are district locations widely visible to the public. Ken-Ton found an answer to the dilemma through one of the schools it has closed as a school but is using as a central facility for district staff development. In one of the larger rooms, where planning teams from the schools are likely to meet, there is a single wall covered with photos of district personnel who have made outstanding contributions toward the district mission of achieving excellence. The pictures are greatly varied, some in color others in black and white, some large others small. No status can be attributed to the differences, however, for administrators, teachers, secretaries, custodians, students, and parents are treated with remarkable equity. This "wall of fame" is exceptionally public and a powerful reminder of what the district values.

Rites of Degradation

Unfortunately, it is sometimes necessary for rites to exist that diminish an individual, reducing his or her status. These *rites of degradation* also play an important part in shaping culture. The classic example in the military is the court martial, followed by a formal stripping of status from the individual, complete with drum rolls in a public ceremony. In the example mentioned earlier in this chapter, teachers were reluctantly transferred to the low-rung school of the district. As such, they were participating in an organizational rite of degradation, even though their behaviors did not warrant it. They had done nothing except to be least senior in the district, yet unconsciously the district was degrading them and sending a message of failure for that school.

In the revitalized Ken-Ton School District, a new ceremonial rite was created that could be either a rite of passage or a rite of degradation. Even though a novice teacher going through the probationary period has a mentor teacher to work with him or her, there are times when the match of that teacher-candidate and the district philosophy is questionable. The teachers association is one of many groups that has a final say in the process. Asking the association to view the candidate as a potential colleague (and to recommend or not recommend) sends an important message about the district's culture. This district values collegiality and teacher empowerment: The voices of teachers will be heard.

Rites Affecting the Organization

The next three rites have both a latent and a manifest function associated with such subgroups as individual schools or departments. The rites not only indicate what the organization values (a latent and symbolic purpose), they also help maintain the viability of the organization (their manifest function).

Rites of Integration

Rites of integration are the ceremonial rites that help bond the organization together, more so than the simple end-of-the-week celebrations at the local pub. In Ken-Ton, these are significant ceremonial affairs that play an important part in transmitting a message.

Whenever there is an all-day meeting of a school's planning team, a lunch is scheduled for the participants and guests at the district's staff development center, where the meeting takes place. Although the lunches are simple, they bring together teachers, administrators, custodians, secretaries, and parents in an informal setting. The message is simple: "Your participation is important to us, we want your continuing involvement." After the first one or two meetings we attended, we actually looked forward to the next lunch, where we could renew acquaintances.

Elaborate rites of much greater significance are those that celebrate success. Whenever a school receives state or national recognition as a School of Excellence, the district holds a grand dinner at the executive dinning room of a downtown bank. The room is well appointed, the

meal lavish (though not extreme), and kudos for the school is high-
lighted. This celebration is for the entire school, the planning team
(which includes parents and business people), school board members,
and administrators. When the first of these were held, the teachers
were surprised; they had not anticipated such a high-quality affair.
That the district took enough pride in the accomplishments of the
school to sponsor an event of this nature permeated the entire system.
When asked about the costs, both school board members and administrators were quick to defend the expenditures: "When we consider
what these teachers have done for our children, the time and effort they
have put into their school and making it what it is today, we think this
simple reward is more than worthwhile." These reward functions have
done much to bond the schools and the district, the educators and the
board, and the district with involved parents.

Rites of Conflict Reduction

Trice and Beyer (1984) give as examples for *rites of conflict reduction*
collective bargaining, arbitration, strikes, committees, and task forces.
They contend that the purpose of such activities is the amelioration of
conflicts and the reduction of aggressive behaviors. By the time Ken-
Ton was into the second stage of the school improvement process, it
had grappled with and created a mechanism for coping with conflict
reduction.

The district recognized that when planning teams got bogged
down with school complaints, they could not fulfill their "vision"
pursuit. Consequently, schools created committees on gripes (COGs).
These committees were problem-solving teams through which internal
school and teacher conflicts could be raised and resolved by generating
ideas to resolve the educational dilemmas.

After the district adopted the |I |D |E |A | framework and this
was "taught" to the schools, COGs became, for most planning teams,
a rite of conflict avoidance. In Chapter 8, we discussed opening meetings with a WHIP (a process that "will help improve participation").
This ritual is symbolic of the total process—it said (to us) that participation of all stakeholders in the school is important and status is not.
Teachers, custodians, administrators, parents, and even guests are
asked to create a WHIP and facilitate it.

There is a demonstrated commitment to equality of power in the
system. Although all administrators are trained as facilitators, meetings themselves are not usually chaired by the principal or assistant

but by a teacher, counselor, or other professional in the school who is also a trained facilitator. Although there are, of course, times when power plays occur, for the most part the |I |D |E |A | meeting rite promotes cohesiveness and high levels of member interaction; the COGs, in turn, fulfill the problem resolution process and thus prohibit conflict from destroying the system.

A second aspect of the meeting rite was an expectation that all members in the planning team will institute a "pyramid of communication." Each member on a planning team was asked to talk with two or three parents and let them know what went on at the meeting, as well as solicit their concerns, questions, or suggestions. These parents in turn were asked to call two or three other parents and inform them, also asking them to call some parents. Theoretically, in about three to five levels almost the entire community can be informed. The process was an experiment in conflict reduction and a symbolic way to keep the community in the know. Although the process initially was attempted, it did not become a viable method (or ceremonial rite) and eventually withered away. Thus all aspects of the |I |D |E |A | process were not always successful, although the attempt to create the system may have been a useful message to the public; it definitely was so for the parents on the teams.

Rites of Renewal

Organizations and their subunits are imperfect creations of humans and cannot be expected always to operate at peak performance. Rites that have the purpose of strengthening or refurbishing the social structure are labeled *rites of renewal*. Trice and Beyer (1984) list as current examples in business and industry such organization development activities as management by objectives, team building, quality circles, job redesign, and survey-feedback interventions. In most school districts, these can be found as staff development activities, such as on "superintendent's days."

In Ken-Ton, staff development was a major focus of the school improvement package, so there were many opportunities for renewal rites to occur. Two examples of "full" rites come to mind.

The superintendent scheduled an annual summer retreat at the staff development center, followed by an informal get together at his home. Initially, school board members and administrators were participants. To reflect the district's changing definition of leader, participation expanded to planning team members, which included staff and parents.

Each retreat had a theme and guest speakers addressing such topics as creativity or total quality management. The sessions were primarily work related, setting expectations or goals for the district, but time was also allocated for informal conversation, cocktails, hors d'oeuvres, and even swimming (weather permitting). Over the course of time, these retreats became widely known and talked about in the system, and subsequently it was considered "very in" to receive an invitation to attend.

Another, more egalitarian, example is a rite that bridged both conflict avoidance and renewal. By the time the third stage of the school improvement process was under way, a systematic evaluation process became fully operational and began to take on the characteristics of an organizational rite. At the end of each year, the school planning teams wanted information to help determine the extent to which they had achieved their goals. They used that information to set targets for the next year and to document the need for resources for working on new goals, as well as those not yet accomplished. The rite went essentially as follows.

At a midsemester spring meeting, the school planning team reviews its goals and hears status reports from the various design teams. Volunteers are sought for the evaluations: one set for developing surveys for teachers, students, and community; a second set for interviewing teachers and students; and a third set for analyzing the parts and synthesizing for a final report. The total planning team then generates sample questions to be considered. These are questions about the goals and processes that were used in the past year, the team designs being implemented, and any new or emerging concerns. Some of the questions generated remain constant from year to year so as to track trends; others change according to the goals or designs.

Next comes the implementation of the evaluations. Teams of two, one to facilitate the session and the second to record the responses, conduct interviews. These are group sessions of all teachers or all students (never were there mixed groups). During the hour-long session, participants share their impressions of the designed projects and vent concerns. The process was strange at first, but after a few years teachers became accustomed to the process. If any find it inhibiting, they can also schedule private sessions or share their concerns through the written surveys that combine open and closed questions.

Third, the analyzed and synthesized results are shared within the planning team. Usually these are reported as percentages for or against a particular item, followed by comments. From these results, the teams begins to make decisions as to whether or not to retain a goal, design a team project, or expand or contract. As participant observers of both planning and design teams, we saw the process unfold and changes occur in both goals and designs.

Fourth, the data and decisions are more broadly shared with the school personnel and eventually with the central administration and school board, as they are the final allocaters of resources.

As this process became somewhat standardized (or ritualized), it became another important culture shaper. It says (as we interpret it) that the organization is not complacent, it realizes projects can fail, it is willing to be open and share both successes and failures, and the system is trying to be self-correcting. It has set a model for teachers, some of whom emulate it in their own classrooms.

Some Concluding Remarks on Organizational Culture

"Organizations exist in a parent culture, and much of what we find in them is derivative from the assumptions of the parent culture" (Schein, 1984, p. 12). What we have done in this chapter is to lift one corner of the cloak of the parent culture of the Ken-Ton district. We have briefly examined the rites and ceremonials as one of the many elements that go into shaping that culture.

Before closing this chapter, we feel compelled to comment on the care needed in planning and implementing rites, rituals, and ceremonies. These symbolic events can work for or against the organization. Bolman and Deal (1995) present a short, fictitious fable about a businessman (Steve) who seeks help from a mentor-consultant (Maria). During the course of his journey, Steve learns about ceremonies as rituals and their use in creating a sense of community. One of the ceremonies Steve tries is meeting workers with a motivational speech about "caring." Steve walks through the shop floor to see employees at their stations and to try his hand at their jobs—after all, this is where he started in the company. (This is an experience akin to a principal, a former teacher, visiting classes and taking one over to demonstrate teaching techniques.) In Steve's case, however, the timing is terrible.

His visit is 6 months after the company has undergone significant downsizing, through which many of the workers lost friends. Before he knows what is happening, Steve is inundated with workers telling him how they felt about "caring." As Steve reflects on the experience, he realizes he was looking to impress the workers and show them there is a common bond—but the workers thought it was a sham. Bolman and Deal's (1995) comments are germane:

> Both ritual and ceremony help us experience the unseen webs of significance that tie a community together. However, when inauthentic, such occasions become meaningless, repetitive, and alienating. They waste time, disconnect us from work, and splinter us from one another. (p. 111)

To make use of organizational rites, with all their nuances, one needs to understand well the central core of beliefs and values (so often unexamined in organizations); to recognize the heroes, the witches, and the storytellers, that is, the authority figures who have shaped and either espouse or deny the core values; and to look at what the organization actions have been, and the peripheral beliefs are—for these are the myths and legends that emanate from the heroes and that communicate the ethos of the organization (Conway, 1985). There are some lessons to be learned about building and changing cultures.

Points to Ponder From the Symbolic Frame

1. It is too obvious to say simply that the use of symbols is important; it is much more than that—it is the very essence for building, sustaining, or transforming a culture supportive of change. Even when there are failures (as in trying to implement pyramids of communication), benefits may accrue. The attempted process of pyramiding was authentic; it demonstrated a genuine valuing of involvement and openness.

2. If rites of enhancement and rites of integration are to be effective, that is, to take on meaning for the system, they should not be approached as token events but should indicate a serious system commitment through a justifiable expenditure of resources. It does not pay to reward richness and quality with frugality.

3. It is a worthwhile activity for administrators and teachers together to look at the kinds of rites (and potential rites) that exist in the system and consider what messages these rites could and should convey. The messages sent are not likely to be overt but rather latent and subtle, and therefore not easily ascertained.

4. Evaluation as a symbolic tool is often overlooked, yet it may be the most important rite a system can develop. It is a powerful shaper of culture for those within the system, as well as for those the system serves.

11

◈

Sustaining Excellence in an Era of Chaos

In Chapters 7 through 10, we interpreted the Kenmore-Town of Tona-wanda (Ken-Ton) Union Free School District's 13-year school improve-ment process from the perspective of four frameworks. We described how Ken-Ton experienced fundamental changes in the basic structural, social, political, and cultural aspects of its organization, using the frameworks to lend a sense of order to the somewhat fragmented, disorderly events and activities within the stages of the change process.

In this chapter, we consider an alternative view using chaos and complexity theory as a point of integration for the preceding chapters to provide insight into a number of characteristics of Ken-Ton's process that have not yet been fully explained. Why was there no centralized master plan, for example, yet there was coherent behavior in the district as a system? Why did some schools fly with innovations, yet others resist change or proceed at a snail's pace? Why, despite the differences, did the improvement initiative produce significant change and ongoing innovation?

In a search for order and predictability in the Ken-Ton experience, one is tempted to try to explain how the seemingly discrete events of each stage of the journey joined together to delineate clear lines of cause and effect. The story of Ken-Ton, however, is a story in which clear-cut connections between cause and effect are lost in the unfolding of events—events that often did not appear to be related to one clear destination or to the planners' foresight and knowledge about how to get there. As such, it represents a form of disorder that reappeared with seeming regularity.

If we look only for order in Ken-Ton's process, we fail to see the true nature of change. Thus, this is not a chapter of conclusions that identify exemplary practices. Rather, it is about new ways of thinking about change.

Chaos and Complexity:
Doing the Obvious Does Not Produce the Obvious

The concepts of *chaos theory* challenge us to develop a new relationship with disorder. The theory suggests that there are no prefixed, definitively describable destinations, that not knowing what is going to matter until the journey is under way is okay. Although a general direction for change may be specified, knowing the steps ahead of time is not important (Wheatley, 1992).

Chaos

The emerging science of chaos is burdened with a misleading name. In normal conversation, the term connotes total randomness, but scientists use it to describe natural systems—from the irregular dripping of a faucet to global weather patterns. Such systems are governed by simple laws yet can evolve into extremely complex, volatile behavior making useful long-term predictions of outcomes impossible (Saperstein & Mayer-Kress, 1988; Waldrop, 1992). Doing the obvious thing may not produce the obvious, desired outcome.

Chaos is also represented by concepts such as *instability, diversity, disequilibrium,* and *complexity* (Popper, 1979). All share the synonym *disorder.* The terms do not connote a complete lack of order or randomness. Rather, they suggest that within chaos is a hidden pattern of order (You, 1993). A major goal of chaos theory is to capture and analyze that apparent disorder (Friedrich, 1989).

Complexity

The new science of chaos is also known as *dynamical systems theory* (Waldrop, 1992, p. 287) and *dynamic complexity* (Senge, 1992). These terms refer to situations where cause and effect are subtle and where the effects over time of interventions are not obvious. For Senge,

> when the same action has dramatically different effects in the short run and the long run, there is dynamic complexity. When an action has one set of consequences locally and a very different set of consequences in another part of a system, there is dynamic complexity. When obvious interventions produce nonobvious consequences, there is dynamic complexity. (p. 71)

The trouble is that we cannot predict exactly when and how such consequences will happen. Educational change, for example, is uncontrollably complex and in many circumstances unknowable (Stacey, 1992). No one can possibly account for all the interactions that figure into a problem or its solution. This is why we need a case study such as that of Ken-Ton. It is a story of dynamic complexity.

Chaos Theory

In a truly complex system, exact patterns are not repeatable yet themes are recognizable (Waldrop, 1992). Chaos theory is an emerging discipline for identifying the structures and patterns that underlie complex situations. The Ken-Ton story, as the study of a complex system, can show us the kinds of patterns we might observe that might be useful to educators and administrators for seeing where actions and changes in structures can lead to significant, enduring improvements.

As a theory, chaos offers a rich language of concepts that help us see deeper—to the patterns lying behind the complex events of the Ken-Ton case. These concepts can help us by restructuring how we think. The theory tells us that reality is made up of circles even though we see straight lines. It reminds us that a small action can snowball. It points out structures that show us that, although everything else in a system may change, some quality always remains the same. Finally, it culminates in a principle that explains why systems at the edge of chaos have their own agenda; that growth is found in chaos not order; and that order, balance, and stability are temporary—that is, we are always on the edge of chaos! The first step is to let go of the notion that cause and effect are close in time and space.

Nonlinearity:
Surprise Is the Norm, Not the Exception

A *linear process* proceeds step by step in a straight line from a particular starting point to a defined end point—the second step cannot be implemented without carrying out the first. The processes of planning and analysis—trying to explain how things work—are examples of a search for order and predictability because we assume that cause and effect are linear, that is, that they are close in time and space. Yet, in spite of the best of plans, we often experience influences we cannot see or test, and strange occurrences pop up everywhere. Doing the obvious thing does not produce the obvious, desired outcome.

Educational systems and events are bound by invisible fabrics of interrelated actions that often take years to play out their effects on each other fully. In Ken-Ton, for example, many critical decisions made throughout the improvement process had systemwide consequences that stretched over a decade. Decisions about staff development influenced and continue to influence what goes on in classrooms. Investing in new technology and instructional strategies influenced the way instruction was delivered. Promoting certain people into principalships shaped strategy and school climate for years.

Situations in which cause and effect are subtle and the long-term effects of interventions are not obvious are *nonlinear* (Senge, 1992). A fundamental characteristic of nonlinear systems is that cause and effect are not closely related in time and space. There are delays between actions and their consequences. It is just such nonlinearity that describes the Ken-Ton process more appropriately than do linear step-by-step flow charts. Change in Ken-Ton did not follow a simple, linear path from analysis of the problem to the design and development of an intervention. Rather, it allowed for adaptations to unexpected or unforeseen contingencies.

It was nearly 5 years before indicators in Ken-Ton could be identified to suggest that the improvement initiative was beginning to make any differences at all. Recall that in the first stage of the school improvement program (SIP), it took 4 years for all schools to achieve fully functioning teams. It took 5 to 8 years before measures of student achievement showed positive upward trends. And it took 10 years for indicators of staff and community morale to show improvement—a full decade to indicate that the district's investment in improvement strategies produced quality results.

Dependence on Initial Conditions: Small Changes, Big Results

In the cliche about the straw that broke the camel's back, a very small change produced a big result. This is also the case in dynamic, complex systems such as school districts. In the language of chaos, this characteristic is called *sensitive dependence on initial conditions*. It means that "the slightest variation in the conditions of a system guarantees that no two outcomes are alike" (Wheatley, 1992, p. 125). Because of sensitivity to initial conditions, studying or tracking a system's behavior over time may allow short-term, but does not guarantee long-term, prediction of its behavior.

This principle expands the notion that often the most obvious solutions do not work by adding that, at best, they may improve things in the short run, only to make things worse in the long run. For example, under budget pressure, administrators often cut back staff to lower costs, but eventually discover their remaining staff are overworked. Eventually, administrators discover that costs have not gone down at all because the work has been farmed out to part-time staff or because overtime has made up the difference.

But there is a corollary. Observers of chaos refer to it as the *principle of leverage* (Gemmill & Smith, 1985; Leifer, 1989; Senge, 1992; Waldrop, 1992; Wheatley, 1992). It suggests that small, well-focused actions can sometimes produce significant, enduring improvement if they are in the right place. Tackling a difficult problem is often a matter of seeing where the locus of high leverage lies—where a change with minimum effort would lead to lasting, significant improvement (Senge, 1992).

Ken-Ton exhibits a host of examples of this principle. In the first stage of the improvement initiative, the introduction of the seemingly simple process of clinical supervision was the catalyst for a variety of shared decision-making mechanisms that would later be the hallmarks of the school improvement process. It set the stage for union-district collaboration (professionalization) and resulted, in the second stage, in contractual alternatives to the formal evaluation of tenured teachers— peer coaching and mentoring—that paved the way for decentralized hiring practices and contractual obligations to shared decision making.

In Chapter 3, we described experiences of the Madison Six team that, at the conclusion of a 5-day off-site training program, decided, "We can make a difference in Kenmore, and we're going to make a difference for kids!" The members returned to the district and proposed that all teachers be trained in the 4-MAT curriculum delivery model. That set a precedent for new structures for staff development. Turnkey training led to the establishment of a teacher center, later to become a staff development center, which was followed by career credits, a radically restructured salary schedule linked to participation in professional development activities.

Also in the second stage, the introduction of a simple process such as monitoring progress toward goals resulted in the larger outcome of reframing and revitalizing the school planning teams. In addition, such a simple thing as involving support staff on planning teams resulted in major improvements in the district's processes and outcomes. Some examples include (1) an employee handbook and orientation video that contributed to improved communication; (2) a safety video produced by transportation staff that involved them in classrooms and in the design of uniform student discipline codes; (3) a mentoring program that improved bus drivers' defensive driving and student management skills; (4) improved purchasing procedures, resulting in cost savings to the district; (5) a self-sustaining food service department; and (6) a computerized cross-department work schedule and work order system that enabled the assigning of service priorities district-wide.

The practice of school self-assessment began with the staff of one school saying to the administration that they would like to apply for a School of Excellence Award. "We think we're good enough. Can you give us substitutes for one day to do the writing?" Out of that came the districtwide expectation that other schools should also apply.

Strange Attractors: Finding the Order in Chaos

Although chaos, in a scientific sense, is not disorder, it suggests that a system is never in the same place twice so it becomes impossible to know where it will be next—there is no predictability (Wheatley, 1992). But if we look at such a system long enough and with the perspective of time, the system does eventually settle down. The system is "magnetically" drawn to certain areas, pulling it into patterns (Briggs & Peat, 1989).

Sensitive dependence on initial conditions shows us that a small action can snowball; however, the concept of strange attractors tells us that limits eventually are encountered. The most chaotic of systems never goes beyond certain boundaries; it stays contained with a shape. Scientists refer to the forces that pull chaotic systems into such patterns as *strange attractors* (Gleick, 1987; Stacey, 1992; Waldrop, 1992; Wheatley, 1992).

Can we identify the force of a strange attractor in organizations? When an attractor is in place, the behaviors of people in the organization are shaped by the attractor, never going out of the bounds of a pattern. Fragmented, disorderly events weave their strands into a pattern—this is the order in chaos (Wheatley, 1992).

When a pattern is identified, it suggests areas of high- and low-leverage change—areas where actions and changes can lead to significant improvements. Leverage in most real-life systems such as school districts is not always obvious to those of us who act in them. Because they are subtle, the patterns and the structures are difficult to see amid the pressures and cross-currents of organizational life. Case studies of organizational transformation, however, provide insight into the kinds of patterns we might observe. Some organizations, tipped into chaos by "permanent white water" or by restructuring, lose their sense of purpose. Others, like Ken-Ton, hold onto a direction in the midst of turbulence. Throughout its 13-year transformation, there were many moments in which the district careened back and forth with disorder. Yet it held onto coherence. Why? Let's look at the Ken-Ton story again in light of its strange attractors.

Patterns in the Ken-Ton Transformation

Following the disorder and chaotic beginnings of its transformation, the district's systems settled down and patterns began repeating themselves. At the end of Chapter 6, Ken-Ton participants described five factors, or patterns, that they called "the whole backbone" of the school improvement process. At least one participant suggested that, "the common thread through all of them is trust." Was that a way of saying that the force—the strange attractor—that shaped new structures and pulled the district's systems into identifiable patterns was trust? Let's reexamine the patterns.

The first factor was the sharing of power by decentralizing hierarchical administrative structures and relationships, empowering informal leaders in all units and at all levels of the district to work collaboratively with formal leaders. One by one, hierarchical aspects of structure fell—from the central office structure to the performance appraisal, compensation, and tenure processes to formally negotiated contracts. All were replaced by consensus-driven teams. Teams had to learn to trust each other and administrators had to learn to trust teams. Informally, participants now reflect that they rarely hear people asking the question, "Who is in charge?" Instead they hear, "Who can you get together to solve these issues?" Similarly, instead of asking "What's wrong?" central administrators more often ask, "How can we help?"

A second pattern was providing structures and supports to help hone skills. Twelve years of unwavering financial commitment to extensive faculty and staff development exemplifies a trust in the centrality of this process. The superintendent's belief in this process is clear: "The board could chip away at any cost it wanted except staff development. I made it clear that I'd throw my body over it first before they took that away."

A third important pattern lay in the development of collaborative relationships among the board, the senior administration, and union leaders. For the past 10 years, union contracts have been informally negotiated "over lunch, with particulars worked out in committees." Critical to this procedural approach is that senior leaders trust one another enough not to abuse the power inherent in sharing knowledge that leaders in many other districts would be hesitant to reveal. A key element is a common willingness to take positions that could be unpopular with respective constituencies.

The fourth critical pattern was the powerful force of experimentation—encouraging risk taking by protecting the freedom to fail. Today in Ken-Ton, faculty continue to use team teaching, mentoring, and peer evaluation without fear that the practices will be used inappropriately for punitive evaluation.

Behind each of these patterns is trust as a strange attractor, as the force that pulled discrete events and activities into patterns that shaped behavior in the district. The patterns suggest areas of high leverage where actions and changes in structure have lead to significant improvement.

Self-Similarity:
The Geometry of Order Within Chaos

Although everything else in a system may change, some qualities remain the same. This universal characteristic of complex nonlinear systems, called *self-similarity,* is derived from a concept in geometry called *fractal scaling.* Self-similarity is the geometry of order within chaos (Mandelbrot, 1983, 1990).

In a fractal structure, the parts of a system have the same qualities as the whole. A familiar example is the toy of nested Russian dolls (Wheatley, 1992). A dominant shape is replicated and is predictable at several smaller levels of scale. Fractals are everywhere in natural systems. The closer we zoom in on a coastline, for example, the more likely the pattern we see at one magnification will be seen at all others. With a few simple guidelines, nature creates the complexity and harmony of form we see everywhere. The same is true for organizations. Wheatley (1992) contends that the best organizations have a fractal quality to them:

> An observer can tell what the organization's values and ways of doing business are by watching anyone, whether it be an employee or a senior manager. There is a consistent and predictability to the quality of behavior. No matter where we look in these organizations self-similarity is found in its people, in spite of the complex range of roles and levels. (p. 132)

There is this same sense in Ken-Ton. While conducting our research, we compared notes with other educators who were acquainted with the district. To a person, we agreed that we could "feel" quality when we walked into a building. In each of the schools, pride and caring about excellence permeated the atmosphere. We tried to identify cues, but none explained the sure sense we had that we, and the students, would be treated well.

The principle of self-similarity—the notion that the parts reflect the whole—provides a useful explanation. Systems are kept in alignment by the capacity for self-similarity. Instead of whirling off in different directions, each part of the system must remain "consistent with itself and with all other parts of the system as it changes" (Wheatley, 1992, p. 146).

The potent force that shapes behavior in fractal organizations is the combination of simply expressed expectations of acceptable behavior and the freedom available to individuals to take risks. These organizations expect to see similar behaviors show up at every level in the organization because such behaviors were patterned into the organization's principles at the very start. A combination of vision and values creates the common identity that connects people and units within such an organization (Wheatley, 1992).

Helfrich described a fractal structure when, at the end of the third stage of the SIP, he described the district as a blob organization (depicted in Figure 5.1). This new organizational structure required making vision and values work in practice. It did not misconstrue organization design as moving around boxes and lines. Rather, the principle of self-similarity—of simple governing principles, guiding visions, and strong values—was at play. The new design required seeing the organization as a system in which the parts are internally connected and it clarified how the whole system could work better.

Senge (1992) tells us that vision is the answer to the question "What do we want to create?" (p. 206). This was the question Ken-Ton was trying to answer in the first stage of its improvement process as it tried to conceptualize what was to be done. When we look carefully, we see that, unlike most visions of one person or group imposed on a district, Ken-Ton's vision was shared. It created a sense of commonality, guided day-to-day problem solving in schools, gave coherence to the diverse visions of individual schools, and was continually being clarified and improved.

Vision painted a picture of what the district wanted to create: excellence. Core values answered the question "How do we want to act along the path toward achieving our vision(s)?" (Senge, 1992, p. 223). Values such as the Nine Principles of Education, shared decision making, and maintaining the identity of schools describe how the district wanted life to be on a day-to-day basis while pursuing the vision.

As individual school teams increasingly took on responsibility for changing and running schools, what was left for senior administrators? One element was stewardship for the district's continually evolving vision and guiding values (Senge, 1992). In the new organizational structure, responsibility for identifying important "commons" and for determining how they should be managed was vested in the central office.

One of Helfrich's chief tasks as a leader was to foster common identity. Much of the leverage he and his administrative team exerted lay in integrating the district's core values and purpose with its operating policies and structures—helping people see the larger explanation of why the district exists and where it was heading.

Self-Organization:
The Path to Order Out of Chaos

In Chapter 7, we described how Ken-Ton, in its struggle to survive in a disruptive and changing (chaotic) environment, creatively transformed itself from a traditional hierarchical organization to a decentralized structure in which decision making is driven by consensus. We showed further, in Chapters 8 through 10, that such transformation involved profound change not only of organizational structure but also in basic social, political, and cultural components. In doing that, the district demonstrated that it was not locked into any one form but had the capacity to create structures that best fit changing requirements. This in turn increased its ability to manage complexity. Throughout the process, however, the district seemed to maintain its identity while changing form. How did it do it? What were the conditions necessary for Ken-Ton's survival in a turbulent and rapidly changing environment? What was the district's path to order out of chaos? What was essential for the district to become and maintain itself as a self-organizing structure?

The principle of self-organization refers to the internal process by which complex systems such as school districts grow and adapt (Jantsch, 1980; Prigogine & Stengers, 1984; Zeleny, 1980). In the world of self-organizing structures, change is not random or incoherent. Instead systems evolve to greater independence and resiliency because they are free to adapt and because, through self-similarity, they maintain a coherent identity throughout their history. Self-organization is a concept that captures and explains the Ken-Ton transformation. In doing so, it is also a point of synthesis for this chapter. In the theory of self-organization, the principles of nonlinearity, sensitive dependence, strange attractors, and fractals are all applied to new ways of understanding change.

From the perspective of self-organization, change does not follow fixed or linear steps, but is better seen as the nonlinear ongoing spiraling process depicted in Figure 11.1. Four characteristics are essential to the process of self organization: (1) trigger points (or disequilibrium), (2) norm-breaking strategies, (3) experimentation, and (4) resynthesis or reformulation (Gemmill & Smith, 1985; Leifer, 1989). There are striking parallels between these characteristics and the stages of the Ken-Ton's transformation. Let's revisit the Ken-Ton story in light of these elements.

Trigger Points

Trigger points are events in a system's environment that overwhelm its capacity to cope—disturbances that signal the need for change. If a disturbance survives the system's attempts to dampen it,

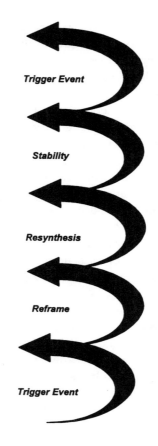

Figure 11.1. The Process of Self-Organization

it grows to the point where it cannot be ignored. It jolts or provokes the system into a response. The organization's survival depends on change (Leifer, 1989; Tichy & Ulrich, 1984). These characteristics describe the conditions in Ken-Ton during the period prior to the beginning of the improvement initiative. Against a backdrop of layoffs, declining staff morale, parental dissatisfaction, and an unsuccessful short-term attempt at school improvement planning, the board of education acknowledged a need "to get back to the business of educating kids as a primary function."

Under such conditions of instability, a system faces a future that is wide open. No one can predict what path it will take. As suggested by the principle of sensitive dependence on initial conditions, creative individuals can have enormous influence under these conditions. Most observers of the transformation process agree that the actual transformation of a system occurs as a consequence of a vision of the organization's future and the will to achieve it (Allaire & Firsirotu, 1985; Meyer, 1982; Quinn, 1985; Tichy & Ulrich, 1984). Recall that in Ken-Ton, what appealed to board members and sold them was Jack Helfrich's ability to "perceive the issues in the district and his ability to provide a vision." Helfrich immediately put a process in place that 13 years later resulted in recognition of the district as a world-class educational organization: small changes, big effects.

During this state of instability in self-organizing systems, change enters the system as a small fluctuation that varies from the flow of normal behavior and expectations. As in the principle of nonlinearity, it's a surprise. An obvious solution does not produce the expected outcome. If the system pays attention to this fluctuation, the change grows. Different parts of the system get hold of it and it grows to the point where it cannot be ignored.

Early in the first stage of Ken-Ton's improvement effort, the building principals, surprised that their usual persistence in stonewalling new initiatives (i.e., quelling system disturbances) did not work, lamented, "They're serious . . . we really are going to do this!" Subsequently, the process amplified itself into a new, unexpected direction for the district, impelled through the creativity of a few principals who, by their successful attempts at change in their own buildings, succeeded in getting the attention of others.

Norm-Breaking Strategies

Norm-breaking strategies refer to overcoming inertia with the help of the new vision. By breaking down existing relationships and habits, something analogous to Lewin's (1947) idea of system unfreezing takes place (Leifer, 1989).

This describes Ken-Ton throughout the first and at the beginning of the second stages of its process. The steps taken by previous superintendents had succeeded in shaking things up, but there had been no follow through, no direction. Helfrich provided a vision and a process. Nevertheless, early on there was minimal consensus, minimal contentment, minimal faith in the new vision and goals for improvement, and minimal consistency in implementing them.

As Helfrich describes it, "Everyone had agreed, 'Yeah, let's get on board and get something done!' but no one really knew yet, exactly what we were agreeing to. We basically agreed to a facilitated change process." In the opinion of a union leader, "We agreed to do something different than we had been doing, but there was no commitment at that time to shared decision making."

Thus, the survival of the initiative depended on rekindling faith in an SIP in which (according to a board member) "half the time we didn't have the vaguest idea where we were going." A teacher puts it another way:

> Here we are, very busy people. We think we're doing our job. We're getting some good results. Then comes the notion of improvement. And people felt inadequate, saying, "You mean I've been doing it wrong all these years?"

From the perspective of self-organization, however, this norm breaking is more than unfreezing; it is more than the breaking down of existing relationships and habits. Rather, it involves the education of system participants in the art of decommitting themselves from existing processes and values (Gemmill & Smith, 1985; Leifer, 1989; Weick, 1977). A Ken-Ton administrator captures the nature of this art when he says, "The change was not about moving the district from bad to good, but from getting us out of a 'maintenance' or status quo mind set."

In the second stage of the SIP, the administrators' bonus system was used to reward administrators whose accomplishments aligned with the improvement initiative. The principal who explains how this worked is also describing the art of decommitting from existing district values:

> The people who got nothing were really upset. But it put the pressure on. More administrators got aboard and started working at it. So it was infectious. Then, as the results started coming in, people who just wanted to renovate their buildings complained that they didn't get the budget they requested. And we said, "Well, you're not doing anything. They're not going to pay you to get new desks."

But the process of decommitting is not easy. Recall the parent who describes it as "kicking and screaming . . . that . . . we don't need this!" And one of the district's consultants reports:

We were advised of certain words that would not be looked on favorably. One of them was "improvement" because it implied that what they were currently doing was not absolutely the best. And it was clear that there was a great deal of pride in the schools held by the "old guard."

Experimentation

Self-organizing systems reorganize themselves around new structures by first experimenting with forms with which they have little experience. This means they are inefficient and require large amounts of energy, resources, and skills (Leifer, 1989). From the end of the first stage throughout the entire second stage and early in the third stage of the SIP, Ken-Ton was in a state of experimentation. The district's vision of shared decision making fostered risk taking and experimentation with such mechanisms as

- *planning teams,* which "learned to complete a cycle of meetings and retreats with no abuses of trust—that is, no one stormed out in protest";
- *peer clinical supervision,* which symbolized a commitment to more autonomy for teachers;
- *the process of monitoring,* which meant "asking tough questions about what we were doing and being prepared to deal with the answers";
- *the teacher center,* which empowered staff to participate in the governance of staff development, and the mentor program, which was "a catalyst to fundamental agreement on the quality of instruction and what ought to be the standard for teachers who will . . . acquire tenure";
- *the Schools of Excellence applications,* which established the expectation that all schools would undergo the process of applying for the award as a means of ongoing self-evaluation; and
- *the career credits option,* which through restructured salary schedules provides the means to reward individual initiative in professional development.

Such experimentation unleashed people's commitment by giving them the freedom to act, to try out their own ideas and be responsible for producing results. An attitude that supported risk taking permeated the district at that time, as reflected in the comments of a teacher who says, "Nobody was criticized if things didn't come out quite the way you thought." This is also stated by the team facilitator who notes, "We weren't afraid to try new ideas . . . instead of saying 'no' they'd say, 'no one can fault you for trying.' " Similarly, a board member comments, "everything started working when people knew they could fail and start again."

But the experimentation was also inefficient. It taxed participants' energy, resources, and skills. It was a time when people were learning from one another. Planning teams developed unevenly—different buildings had different levels of success. Those that were quicker to take risks moved ahead rapidly. A principal suggests that in the beginning, because few teams dealt with curricular issues or fundamental restructuring of "what kids do in schools," it was easy to get consensus about "improving the cafeteria for both students and faculty . . . but as you get into things more substantial, you have more potential for disagreement."

Once the transformation has caught on, a self-organizing system stabilizes and learns to be more efficient. Ken-Ton's transformative process is an acknowledgment, however, that the new states of order are not comfortable, stable ones in which the system easily stays until disturbed again. Rather, they are difficult to sustain because they require continual inputs of energy if they are to survive (Stacey, 1992). Ken-Ton, suffering from disorder and chaos at the outset of its journey, required an infusion of energy just to maintain itself. Initiating a process of change required even more energy. Effort was required to move people, technology, and systems beyond inertia into uncharted and undiscovered areas. Work was necessary not simply to get people to change their habits and routines, but to get them to decommit from what they knew to be true and to trust in a destination that was not yet fully known.

It took energy to get people to trust. Part of that infusion of energy came in the form of money (career credits, paying for attending team meetings, celebrations of success), as a conscious realization that "we couldn't ask people to commit to the degree we were asking for 'nothing.' " Administrators discovered their intentions as they moved through time rather than setting them well in advance as stable guides for action. Nevertheless, new order was produced as the result of high levels of cooperation and risk taking, as well as a result of embracing disorder as an opportunity to experiment.

Reformulation (at a Higher Level)

Self-organizing systems try out new structures until they find a preferred one, one in which dissonance is resolved and a new view reframes what is considered to be true (Quinn & Cameron, 1986).

In Ken-Ton, by the end of the second stage, the stage of buy-in, staff had committed themselves to making the vision of shared decision making real. But it was not until the third stage—8 years into the process—that the vision became a living force and staff felt ownership. Participants' examples that shared decision making had become standard practice provide evidence that conflicts had been resolved: "The way we hire people, the way we determine whether teachers receive tenure, the way we determine what the goals of a building are going to be—it's all done by shared decision making." A union leader comments, "It had become a way of life—the way things are done now." And a board member provides evidence that what was formerly considered to be true had been reframed when she says, "It's no longer part of the school improvement effort. Rather, it's so deeply ingrained that it's just the way we do business. We take it for granted now."

In this phase of the self-organization process, the change from one state to another appears to be an orchestrated, simultaneous leap. But what is at work is a whole system creating the conditions that lead to the sudden jump. Change builds on change and the system makes rapid transitions to a new state. This perception was the case in Ken-Ton. The district referred to it as "achieving critical mass" or "just the way we do business now."

It is in this state of reformulation that the chaos principles of strange attractors and self-similarity apply. Note that in self-organization, the whole system reorganizes around a preferred structure, which implies that the system parts become attracted to a new configuration. Moreover, the preferred structure is not just a random rearrangement of parts, it is consistent with the system's prior history (Gemmill & Smith, 1985). That is, it is self-similar.

The new system can maintain its overall character and identity while better managing the complexity of its environment because each part of the system is free to express itself within the context of the history, values, and traditions of the whole. In Ken-Ton, this is demonstrated in the blob organization structure.

At the heart of the system (depicted in Figure 5.1) are teaching-learning teams, surrounded horizontally by teams of traditional decision makers and power brokers who assume roles of facilitation, support, and celebration. The principle of self-similarity is evidenced in the superintendent's response to the criticism that, according to the diagram, no one seems to be in charge:

> In a consensus-driven model no one is in charge because everyone affected by a decision has had a direct or indirect role in its development, is willing to support it, and will therefore be accountable for results. Failed outcomes or goals are something to be corrected and learned from. Blame, disguised as accountability and defined by clear lines of authority which add layers of individuals who can start or stop a process at any level, is not an essential component of this model.

In this statement, self-similarity is enhanced with a few simple guidelines and rules that now guide all levels of the district's operation, derived from a clear sense of identity grounded in values, traditions, aspirations, competencies, and culture.

Recycle

In the theory of self-organization, the state of reformulation is followed by a period of stability and adaptation until the process recycles with a trigger event that signals the need for change once again.

Although the Ken-Ton story is incomplete (evolving even as it is being told in this book), we see hints of disequilibrium beginning again in the fourth stage of the journey. The Excelsior Award spun the district in a new direction. Although consistent with the Ken-Ton vision of excellence, it set an agenda that suggests the district is struggling with a number of issues that point to the tentativeness of the new structures. Among them are achieving control without controlling individual schools; increasing coordination and collaboration among schools; cascading the tools of quality from the organizational to the classroom level; and restructuring the teaching-learning process. Other challenges include the problem of integrating new members of the school community into the district's culture of shared decision making as the superintendent who guided the process retires and retirement incentives continue to reduce the number of members who have "lived" the process. An even greater challenge is the changing demographics of the community.

Summary:
The Lessons in Chaos

School districts are complex systems where the scale of complexity is without precedent. In the Ken-Ton case, the district and its schools were implementing a bewildering array of multiple innovations and policies simultaneously. Restructuring reforms were so multifaceted and complex that solutions for particular settings could not be known in advance. Doing the obvious thing did not necessarily produce the obvious, desired outcome. There were many situations where cause and effect were subtle, the effects over time of interventions were not obvious, and the same action had one set of consequences in one school and a very different set of consequences in another part of the district.

How can knowledge of chaos concepts help administrators be more successful in such complex systems? Such knowledge provides insight into some practical problems and core dilemmas such as

- how we maneuver in an environment of uncertainty;
- how we learn from experience when often the consequences of our most important decisions are in the future or in a remote part of the system;
- how we know what is important to focus on and what needs less attention;
- how a district can distribute decision-making responsibility widely and still retain coordination and control; and
- the nature of the commitment and competencies required to manage the disorder that accompanies improving education systems.

As the pace and intensity of educational change continues to create conditions where traditional coping mechanisms do not work, the language of chaos takes on increased importance. As we begin to understand it through its application to the Ken-Ton case, we gain an appreciation for the power of leverage in managing change—seeing where actions and changes in structures can lead to significant, lasting improvement. Administrators, however, often focus on low-leverage change—on symptoms where the stress is greatest. The language of chaos points to five tools for helping administrators distinguish high- from low-leverage changes in highly complex situations.

1. The concept of nonlinearity teaches that there is leverage in accept- ing that we cannot fully predict or guide change with any precision. For administrators, this suggests "keeping options open by going for something workable, rather than what's optimal" (Waldrop, 1992, p. 333). In the case of Ken-Ton, it meant settling initially for low-risk, high-visibility improvement projects rather than demand- ing projects that immediately made a difference in student learning.

2. The principle of sensitive dependence on initial conditions suggests that there is little leverage in acting on the most obvious symptoms of problems. It may not lead to lasting improvements. Or symptoms may improve in the short run, only to get worse in the long run because small actions can snowball. The principle of leverage, on the other hand, suggests that small changes can produce big results if they are in the right place. Tackling a difficult problem is often a matter of seeing a change that, with a minimum of effort, may lead to lasting, significant improvement.

3. The concept of strange attractors teaches that there is leverage in seeing patterns. But leverage, in most real-life systems such as school districts, is not obvious to most of the actors in those systems. The art of finding strange attractors lies in seeing through disorder and chaos to the underlying patterns, rather than seeing only events and forces to react to. As the study of a complex system, the Ken-Ton case shows the kinds of patterns we might observe.

4. The capacity for self-similarity is asking us to develop a different understanding of autonomy. It suggests that much of the leverage administrators can exert lies in trusting simple governing rules and guidelines. The leverage Helfrich and his administrative team ex- erted lay in integrating the district's core values and purpose with its operating policies and structures. The combination of vision and values forms the common identity that connects people and schools within a district. The administrator's task is to communicate vision and values, to keep them ever-present and clear and then allow individuals in the system to experiment. This is no easy task. Such experimentation may appear to be chaotic. What makes this princi- ple difficult to practice is that administrators' training and experi-

ences urge them to interfere, to stabilize apparent chaos and shore things up. But it is not necessary to crush chaos to get rid of it. If administrators maintain clarity about the purpose and direction of their district or school, order is more likely to be maintained.

5. Yet another important teaching aid for administrators is in the behavior of self-organizing systems. The Ken-Ton journey, evidence that the ability of such systems to break norms, to experiment, and to reorganize, suggests that a district that successfully transforms itself is one that develops high levels of cooperative behavior, promotes risk taking, and embraces disorder as an opportunity to experiment.

12

❖

Epilogue

The Never-Ending Story of Change Continues

We would be remiss if we did not relate what happened in the Ken-more-Town of Tonawanda (Ken-Ton) Union Free School District after the retirement of Superintendent Jack Helfrich. There are so many questions that come to mind about the aftermath. Who replaced the retiring superintendent and what was the process for selection? Has the district continued to grow or is it stagnant? Has the community continued to support the changes that were begun and the costs associated with staff development, mentoring, and the fiscal initiatives? Has the district continued its quest for excellence? Is it capitalizing on the initial thrust of the | I | D | E | A | framework or has it replaced that with another framework and related initiative? If readers are to make judgments as to the efficacy of the processes described in Part I, then they will need to know what worlds the 13-year sojourn has found (or created). To help readers make their assessments, we briefly examine the developments that have occurred in the district since the retirement of two of the program's major champions: the superintendent and the deputy superintendent.

Developments in the Intervening Years

The last year of Helfrich's superintendency was somewhat traumatic for the school district. The board of education and teachers did not want to lose what many saw as the driving force for the district's position of excellence. The superintendent, on the other hand, was convinced that leadership permeated the entire district and it was ready for a replacement. He told his colleagues and his board that

Ken-Ton had not come to its present position on the shoulders of one person, but rather it had adopted a process for change that was not likely to be extinguished. Nevertheless, this was another change that the district had to face. Not only was the superintendent leaving, but the deputy superintendent who had facilitated the school improvement program (SIP) for 13 years was also announcing his retirement. In addition, a long-time personnel administrator had recently left. In essence, almost the entire core leadership of the central office was going to be replaced.

The transition year was aided by the deputy agreeing to stay on as acting superintendent while a search committee went into action. The committee, aided by an outside consultant, advertised the position nationally and was able to narrow the applications to three highly qualified candidates. The three were superintendents with outstanding reputations, rightfully so, as Ken-Ton was well recognized for its support for education. Each came to the interviews with well-thought-out strategies for moving the district. They were experienced persons with strength in strategic planning and commensurate management skills. After meeting all candidates and going through much deliberation, the board decided to continue the search rather than hire any of the finalists. The board was not negative about the finalists; all were excellent. Rather, it believed that the finalists did not match well with the direction that the school system had taken.

The board commissioned the consultant to take a proactive stance and generate more candidates for consideration. That process provided a totally new pool that was again narrowed to a short list for interviews. This time, the finalists were not yet superintendents, though all were experienced administrators.

The short list was particularly interesting in that it seemed to send a message that the district was not looking for a "new" system, a replacement for the I I I D I E I A I framework, but wanted a person who would grow with the current process. Well-established superintendents were rejected for a person who had not yet been so shaped by experiences that he or she would be prescriptive. The district's "want list" was headed by such qualities as compatibility with the board, a genuine concern for people, and, most important, an individual open to learning the Ken-Ton process. Robert McClure, who had been deputy superintendent in a suburb of Rochester, New York, a system approximately 80 miles east of Buffalo, was selected as superintendent. In the board's judgment, McClure matched the want list well. His background included process training similar to the |I |D |E |A | processes, and 6 years of experience in implementing a philosophy of involvement that was reasonably congruent with the Ken-Ton approach to school improvement.

During the first months of McClure's tenure, he attended the |I |D |E |A | training, sending a message to the district that this was something he was willing to learn and would continue to support. Many school districts have a problem of too much rather than too little change. Both schools and districts begin projects and often find the projects wither away, either from changes in board membership that result in reduced financial support or from changes in administrative leadership where the philosophy or the knowledge base and related values of the replacement administrator are not compatible with what has been begun.

Soon after McClure was in office, the district began a second major search, a replacement for the retiring deputy superintendent for curriculum and instruction. The applicants for this position were as numerous as for the superintendency. Criteria for the position were generated by soliciting expectations from a variety of focus groups: students, parents, support staff, administrators, teacher association, and board of education groups. There was an exceptionally high congruency of expectations across the groups so that a well-defined profile emerged.

Once again, a short list was generated; after extensive interviews, Fred Morton looked most promising. Morton was not a stranger to Ken-Ton. He had conducted training in the district as far back as 1988, which was about the time he had left a principalship to become a full-time |I |D |E |A | consultant. He impressed the district with his knowledge about learning, his skills in working with people, and his extensive experiences in administrative posts at all levels from elementary through high school.

The symbolic messages associated with his appointment were significant. The obvious message was the intent to continue the |I |D |E |A | process thrust; less obvious, but even more significant, was a change in the title of the position to assistant superintendent for curriculum, instruction, and learning. The addition of the word "learning" was a deliberate move to emphasize the district's concern for life-long learning not only as an outcome for students but equally as a valued process to be modeled by teachers, administrators, and board members. It signaled a concern that the new person would be involved with creating environments and nurturing support at all levels of the system and for all parts of the organization.

As we reflect on the 13-year history of the school improvement process and the new leadership, our question is whether or not the district will continue to advance. We have distinct feelings that it is in good hands, but we want the readers to have an opportunity to decide that for themselves.

You Be the Judge

In November 1995, 1 year after the hiring of the new superintendent, we revisited the district. We interviewed the new superintendent, Robert McClure, and his newly hired deputy, Fred Morton. Below, we provide portions of our dialogues with each of them. As you eavesdrop on our conversations, you be the judge. Have the values of the improvement process been sustained? Has leadership been built in? Will the quality process continue?

Excerpts From an Interview With Superintendent Robert McClure

JC/JS   Given this district's history, how do you see your role?

RM   My answer will be somewhat obscure. . . . At a retreat this fall, members of the board of education targeted a goal—to improve its communications. Last night, as a follow-up to the retreat, Fred and I facilitated a working session of the board designed to further define that goal. We asked them first to "think of an organization you've done business with in the past that you would recommend to others because you were fully satisfied as a customer. . . . What made you satisfied?"

The meeting was open to the public and a news reporter who was there didn't understand what was going on. I turned to him and said, "They're learning!" And indeed they were learning! They were modeling life-long learning. That's part of my role, it's what I call "walking the talk."

What gets lost in the day-to-day running of schools is validating the kinds of assumptions we are all prone to make. For example, we may have to define and verify customer requirements. The next step is to figure out how to verify with parents and the community what we think we know. To do that we'll probably use some form of Pareto diagram. . . . I mentioned this process to a few principals and they wanted a copy. Now, everyone is using it!

What Jack [Helfrich] said about leadership being built in here is true . . . the success of the district is not on the shoulders of one person . . . everyone understands their job is to be a leader, facilitator, and supporter, depending on the situation.

JC/JS Where do you want this district to go? What difference do you want to make?

RM I spent the first year meeting people. Everywhere I was asked, "What is the vision?" My response was, "If you're looking for a white knight, you know you'd be disappointed. We have to take a look collectively at what it is . . . and we have to include more of the community." You can't walk into this district with a canned program and have anyone buy it!

I much prefer that the changes we make be a mandate that comes from the community. . . . The WHAT needs to be decided on by the community in concert with us. It's not up to educators alone to decide.

Last summer's retreat we expanded to include more of the community. We made a concrete effort to bring in business, industry, and higher education. There's a huge gap in terms of their view of what we're training kids to do. . . . We invited them to present their views . . . we talked about the difficulty of change. We did the majority of the listening. We found out we had a lot more in common than differences. We asked them what kids need to do or be in order to survive. . . . The break-out groups sent back the following list:

- Lifelong learners
- Good communicators (listening)
- Problem solvers (life doesn't ask multiple-choice questions)
- Technology literate
- Critical thinkers
- Basic skills

Anything that educators would put on the list was there! It planted the idea that we're going to do what they want us to do, not what we think is right. One result of the retreat is they're going to allow us into companies to do turnkey training with their staff. . . . The next stage is to define what the things on that list mean.

For a future retreat, we'll invite graduates to come back and ask them "Here's what business and industry said. Here's what higher education said. You've been out there. Now it's your turn to tell us."

I also go out in the community. Recently I spoke to the Rotary. Instead of talking political issues and tax bases, I talked about my passion—about what I do and how we need business and industry to help us. I asked them what they think kids need in the future. I handed out a worksheet, asked them to create a list and to sign their name if they wanted to get the results. Next, we have to target other audiences. You don't gain communitywide support by going to two meetings and think it's over!

I don't want to go backwards. People have asked me why follow a legend (i.e., Helfrich)? I say why not? I came from a district where things were going well. . . . I'm not interested in "saving a sinking ship."

JC/JS   What about acclimating staff who are new to this culture?

RM   With the retirement incentives, we've had a huge turnover in staff. So, one thing we've done is to expand new teacher orientation from 1½ days to 1 week! We put in a component on the history of the district and we will incorporate a portion of Level 1 facilitator training. Another piece is the mentor program. We're the only district that has full-time release for mentors. The program is going strong. The designers were clever. They kept the starting salary low.

JC/JS   What about intervening with experienced teachers in instructional difficulty?

RM   I groan when I hear people say nothing can be done. It can be done! You put it to them in terms of "instructionally here's what I don't see happening . . ." then develop a one-on-one personal plan . . . All teachers strive to improve.

JC/JS   The district's demographics, how are they changing?

RM   We're growing by over 100 students per year—they are from
        a cross-section, not just the inner city—but we will not be
        building new schools. We have been leasing the closed ones
        and will reopen one, perhaps for an alternative school. Right
        now we have alternative school programs with BOCES. I
        visited all of them and talked to our kids. That doesn't
        happen regularly.

JC/JS   How is the search progressing for more sophisticated data-
        gathering mechanisms to track success?

RM   We are beyond attitudinal questions. Now we are asking
        "Are we making a difference?" We want to know the results
        of our efforts. . . . You measure what you value . . . what does
        the community value? The PEP test doesn't tell you about
        problem solving and critical thinking.

        Studies on effective organizations other than schools
        are now describing their fractal quality, which means that
        anywhere you go you see consistency of how people oper-
        ate . . . what they value. When we start to define what kids
        need, we are also defining how we must operate as adults.
        . . . If we expect kids to be problem solvers, we must model
        problem solving.

        But the principals ask, "If we get rid of the old and bring
        the new we have to show the public it's making a difference
        . . . why shouldn't we use it for accountability . . . how else
        do we know?" For example, we use the Comprehensive
        Assessment Report only as a baseline. It doesn't measure
        what we value. We have to go beyond what it presents to
        highlight publicly what schools are doing.

        Two buildings, for example, are measuring exciting
        things . . . in one, the principal is doing 4-MAT and learning
        styles. She has information on changes in student outcomes
        that go beyond adult perceptions. . . . Three buildings have
        new report cards. I went to a meeting with them last sum-
        mer. It was 106 degrees and they were not getting paid, so I
        knew they were committed! They asked for a waiver from
        the district report card. I said, "Sure, if you can sell me!" I
        asked if there were any parents at the meeting? They said,
        "No, we're waiting." I said, " I think you've made a mistake.

They probably want to be here now. Call 10 or 12. Ask them to come in. Have them help you present it at open house." That's an example of how we have to take what we already know about working with groups and apply it.

Later I spoke to a parents group at those schools. It actually turned out that the parents whose kids were not in the pilot group for new report cards were the most upset.

JC/JS What kind of restructuring is under way?

RM   In one case, one of the high schools requested a double English period. I asked, "Why is it important to change the structure? What's happening in the current structure? How conceptually are we getting kids to think? Are you aligned with the district's goals? Does it tie in to what the district says is important and what the community has validated?" The focus now is "What's happening when kids are in class?"

***Excerpts From an Interview With Fred Morton,
Ken-Ton Deputy Superintendent for
Curriculum, Instruction, and Learning***

JC/JS What is the next step for the district, as you see it?

FM   The focus is beginning to drift from vision-as-the-driver back to problem solving. For example, if what a team hears from monitoring is day-to-day stuff and if there's no vehicle to refer it to, the tendency is for the planning team to handle it. We need to bring people together to look at that. Not to bring in new processes. Rather, the existing ones need to be recommitted. The challenge is how to ensure the processes broaden across the district. That is, using them to integrate goals so they connect more closely and deeply with what's going on in classrooms.

JC/JS What goals have you set?

FM   Each Friday I look at my calendar for two places in the following week to spend time in a school. To meet each time with the principal and planning team and ask, "What does the curriculum look like to you? How does it fit with the improvement process? How is the planning team working?

Is it shifting to problem solving? Do we need to analyze meetings? How can the planning team be reengaged and expanded to get more of the community involved?"

Long range we need to do advanced facilitation work. It's been 8 years since most people took the training and 30% to 40% of the material has changed.

Conclusion

Gardner (1995) contends that all successful leaders must confront six enduring features or themes:

A leader is likely to achieve success only if she can construct and convincingly communicate a clear and persuasive story; appreciate the nature of the audience(s), including its change-able features; invest her own (or channel others') energy in the building and maintenance of an organization; embody in her own life the principal contours of the story; either provide direct leadership or find a way to achieve influence through indirect means; and, finally, find a way to understand and make use of, without being overwhelmed by, technical ex-pertise. (p. 302)

As we think back on the 13-year school improvement process and as we analyze the words of the new leadership in Ken-Ton, we feel optimistic about concluding that the district has had, and will continue to have, a cadre of administrators, parents, board members, teachers, and staff members who manifest the elements of successful leaders. But only time will tell.

And so the journey continues . . .

References

Ackoff, R. (1974). *Redesigning the future: A systems approach to social problems.* New York: John Wiley.

Allaire, Y., & Firsirotu, M. (1985). How to implement radical strategies in large organizations. *Sloan Management Review, 62*(3), 19-34.

Argyris, C., & Schon, D. (1978). *Organizational learning.* Reading, MA: Addison-Wesley.

Bacharach, S. B., & Mundell, B. L. (1993). Organizational politics in schools: Micro, macro, and logics of action. *Educational Administration Quarterly, 29*(4), 423-452.

Bartunek, J., & Moch, M. (1987). First-order, second-order, and third-order change and organization development interventions: A cognitive approach. *Journal of Applied Behavioral Science, 23*(4), 483-500.

Berman, P., & McLaughlin, M. (1978. *Federal programs supporting education change: Implementing and sustaining innovations* (Report No. R-1589/8-HEW). Santa Monica, CA: RAND.

Bolman, L. G., & Deal, T. E. (1991). *Reframing organizations: Artistry, choice, and leadership.* San Francisco: Jossey Bass.

Bolman, L. G., & Deal, T. E. (1993). Everyday epistemology in school leadership: Patterns and prospects. In P. Hallinger, K. Leithwood, & J. Murphy (Eds.), *Cognitive perspectives in educational leadership* (pp. 21-33). New York: Teachers College Press.

Bolman, L. G., & Deal, T. E. (1994). Looking for leadership: Another search party's report. *Educational Administration Quarterly, 30*(1), 77-96.

Bolman, L. G., & Deal, T. E. (1995). *Leading with soul: An uncommon journey of spirit.* San Francisco: Jossey-Bass.

Boulding, K. (1964). General systems as a point of view. In M. D. Mesarovic (Ed.), *Views on general systems theory* (pp. 25-38). New York: John Wiley.

Briggs, J., & Peat, F. D. (1989). *Turbulent mirror: An illustrated guide to chaos theory and the science of wholeness.* New York: Harper & Row.

Burns, J. M. (1978). *Leadership.* New York: Harper & Row.

Calzi, F., & Conway, J. A. (1995). *Status of shared decision making in Western New York. Report for Erie-Niagara School Superintendents Association.* (Mimeo)

Cetron, M., & Gayle, M. (1991). *Educational renaissance: Our schools at the turn of the century.* New York: St. Martin's.

Conger, J. A. (1989). *The charismatic leader.* San Francisco: Jossey-Bass.

Conway, J. A. (1984). The myth, mystery and mastery of participative decision making in education. *Educational Administration Quarterly, 20*(3), 1-40.

Conway, J. A. (1985). A perspective on organizational cultures and organizational belief structure. *Educational Administration Quarterly, 21*(4), 7-25.

Conway, J. A. (1990) Organizational rites as culture markers for schools. *Urban Education, 25*(1), 195-206.

Conway, J. A., & Calzi, F. (1995/1996). The dark side of shared decision making. *Educational Leadership, 53*(4), 45-49.

Covey, S. R. (1989). *The seven habits of highly effective people.* New York: Simon & Schuster.

Crosby, P. (1979). *Quality is free.* New York: Mentor/New American.

Dachler, H. P., & Wilpert, B. (1978). Conceptual dimensions and boundaries of participation in organizations: A critical evaluation. *Administrative Science Quarterly, 23*(1), 1-39.

Deal, T. E. (1985). Cultural change: Opportunity, silent killer, or metamorphosis? In R. Kilmann, M. Saxton, & R. Serpa (Eds.), *Gaining control of the corporate culture* (pp. 292-331). San Francisco: Jossey-Bass.

Deal, T. E., & Peterson, D. (1990). *The principal's role in shaping a school culture.* Washington, DC: U.S. Department of Education, Office of Educational Research and Development.

Deming, W. (1982). *Quality, productivity, and competitive position.* Cambridge: Massachusetts Institute of Technology Center for Advanced Engineering Study.

Deming, W. (1986). *Out of the crisis.* Cambridge: Massachusetts Institute of Technology Center for Advanced Engineering Study.

Doremus, R. R. (1982). What ever happened to . . . Wayland (Mass.) high school? *Phi Delta Kappan, 63*(5), 347-348.

Edmonds, R. (1979). Effective schools for the urban poor. *Educational Leadership, 37*(1), 15-24.

Eisner, E. W. (1991). *The enlightened eye.* New York: Macmillan.

Eisner, E. W. (1994). *The educational imagination: On the design and evaluation of school programs* (3rd ed.). New York: Macmillan.

Enochs, J. C. (1981). Up from management. *Phi Delta Kappan, 63*(2), 175-178.

Feigenbaum, A. (1983). *Total quality control.* New York: McGraw-Hill.

Firestone, W., & Corbett, H. (1988). Planned organizational change. In N. J. Boyan (Ed.), *Handbook in Research in Education* (pp. 321-340). White Plains, NY: Longman.

Friedrich, P. (1989). Eerie chaos and eerier order. *Journal of Anthropological Research, 44*(4), 435-444.

Gabor, A. (1990). *The man who discovered quality.* New York: Random House.

Gardner, H. (1995). *Leading minds: An anatomy of leadership.* New York: Basic Books.

Gemmill, G., & Smith, C. (1985). A dissipative structure model of organization transformation. *Human Relations, 38*(8), 751-766.

Gleick, J. (1987). *Chaos: Making a new science.* New York: Penguin.

Glickman, C.D. (1990). Pushing school reform to a new edge: The seven ironies of school empowerment. *Phi Delta Kappan, 72*(1), 68-75.

Goffman, I. (1974). *Frame analysis.* New York: Harper.

Goldhammer, R. (1969). *Clinical supervision and special methods for the supervision of teachers.* New York: Holt, Rinehart & Winston.

Golembiewski, R., Billingsley, K., & Yeager, S. (1976). Measuring change and persistence in human affairs: Types of change generated by OD designs. *Journal of Applied Behavioral Science, 12*(2), 133-157.

Goodlad, J. (1975). *The dynamics of educational change.* New York: McGraw-Hill.

Greenleaf, R. K. (1977). *Servant leadership: A journey into the nature of legitimate power and greatness.* New York: Paulist.

Hart, A. W. (1993). *Principal succession: Establishing leadership in schools.* Albany: SUNY Press.

Hersey, P., & Blanchard, K. H. (1977). *The management of organizational behavior* (3rd ed.). Englewood Cliffs, NJ: Prentice Hall.

Hesse, H. (1956). *Journey to the east* (H. Rosner, Trans.). New York: Farrar, Straus & Giroux.

Holmes , E. (1992). Leadership in the quest for quality. *Issues & Observations, 12*(3), 5-7.

Hunt, J. G. (1984). Organizational leadership: The contingency paradigm and its challenges. In B. Kellerman (Ed.), *Leadership: Multidisciplinary perspectives* (pp. 113-138). Englewood Cliffs, NJ: Prentice Hall.

Imai, M. (1986). *Kaizen: The key to Japanese competitive success*. New York: McGraw-Hill.

Institute for Development of Educational Activities (I I I D I E I A I). (1993). *Overview of school improvement*. Dayton, OH: Author.

Ishikawa, K. (1985). *What is total quality control? The Japanese way*. Englewood Cliffs, NJ: Prentice Hall.

Jantsch, E. (1980). *The self-organizing universe*. New York: George Braziller.

Joyce, B., & Showers, S. (1980). Improving inservice training: The messages of research. *Educational Leadership, 37*, 370-385.

Juran, J. (1974). *Quality control handbook*. New York: McGraw-Hill.

Katz, D., & Kahn, R. L. (1966). *The social psychology of organizations*. New York: John Wiley.

Keasling, W. (Ed.). (1992). *The Kenmore-Town of Tonawanda Union Free School District New York State Governor's Excelsior Award Application*. Kenmore-Town, NY: Kenmore-Town of Tonawanda Union Free School District.

Kelley, R. E. (1992). *The power of followership*. New York: Doubleday Currency.

Kolb, D. (1974). *Organizational psychology: A book of readings* (2nd ed.). Englewood Cliffs, NJ: Prentice Hall.

Kolb, D. (1985). *Learning style inventory*. Boston: McBer.

Kowalski, T., & Reitzug, U. (1993). *Contemporary school administration*. New York: Longman.

Kuhn, (1970). *The structure of scientific revolutions*. Chicago: University of Chicago Press.

Leifer, R. (1989). Understanding organizational transformation using a dissipative structure model. *Human Relations, 42*(10), 899-916.

Lewin, K. (1947). Frontiers in group dynamics, part 2: Channels of group life: Social planning and action research. *Human Relations, 1*, 143-153.

Locke, E. A., & Schweiger, D. A. (1979). Participation in decision-making: One more look. In B. M. Staw (Ed.), *Research in organizational behavior* (Vol. 1, pp. 265-339). Greenwich, CT: JAI.

Mandelbrot, B. (1983). *The fractal geometry of nature*. New York: Freeman.

Mandelbrot, B. (1990). Fractals: A geometry of nature. *New Scientist, 1271*(734), 38-43.

Markus, H., & Zajonc, R. (1985). The cognitive perspective in social psychology. In G. Lindzey & E. Aronson (Eds.), *The handbook of social psychology* (Vol. 1, pp. 137-230). New York: Random House.

McCarthy, B. (1980). *The 4Mat System: Teaching to learning styles with right/left mode techniques*. Oak Brook, IL: Excel.

McCarthy, B. (1985). *The 4Mat System: A cycle of learning*. Barrington, IL: Excel.

Meyer, A. (1982). Adapting to environmental jolts. *Administrative Science Quarterly, 27*, 515-537.

Miller, J. (1989). *Transferring teaching skills and strategies from the inservice workshop into practice in the classroom: An evaluation of one district's experience* (Dissertation Abstracts International, 8919358). Doctoral dissertation. State University of New York at Buffalo.

Mintzberg, H. (1979). *The structuring of organizations: A synthesis of the research.* Englewood Cliffs, NJ: Prentice Hall.

Mintzberg, H. (1983). *Structure in fives: Designing effective organizations.* Englewood Cliffs, NJ: Prentice Hall.

Mintzberg, H. (1989). *Mintzberg on management: Inside our strange world of organizations.* New York: Free Press.

Nyberg, D. (1990). Power, empowerment and educational authority. In S. Jacobson & J. A. Conway (Eds.), *Educational leadership in an age of reform* (pp. 49-64). New York: Longman.

Orwell, G. (1946). *Shooting an elephant and other stories.* New York: Harcourt Brace Jovanovich.

Pfeffer, J. (1994). *Managing with power: Politics and influence in organizations.* Boston, MA: Harvard Business School Press.

Popper, K. (1979). *Objective knowledge.* London: Oxford University Press.

Prigogine, I., & Stengers, I. (1984). *Order out of chaos: Man's new dialogue with nature.* New York: Bantam.

Quinn, J. B. (1985). Managing innovation: Controlled chaos. *Harvard Business Review, 63*(3), 73-84.

Quinn, R. E., & Cameron, K. (1986, August). *The transformational cycle: A dynamic theory of excellence.* Paper presented at the Academy of Management Annual Meeting, Chicago.

Rost, J. C. (1993). *Leadership for the twenty-first century.* Westport, CT: Praeger.

Saperstein, A., & Mayer-Kress, G. (1988, December). A nonlinear dynamical model of the impact of SDI on the arms race. *Journal of Conflict Resolution, 32*(4), 636-670.

Sarason, S. (1971). *The culture of the school and the problem of change.* Boston: Allyn & Bacon.

Schein, E. H. (1984). Coming to a new awareness of organizational culture. *Sloan Management Review, 25*(3), 3-16.

Schein, E. H. (1986). A critical look at current career development and research. In E. T. Hall & Associates (Eds.), *Career development in organizations* (pp. 310-331). San Francisco: Jossey-Bass.

Schmuck, R., & Miles, M. (1971). *Organization development in schools.* New York: McGraw-Hill.

Schwartz, H., & Davis, S. M. (1981). Matching corporate culture and business strategy. *Organizational Dynamics, 9*(1), 30-48.

Senge, P. M. (1992). *The fifth discipline: The art and practice of the learning organization.* New York: Doubleday.

Shipengrover, J. (1994). *The relationship of total quality management to the implementation of the school improvement process in a New York State Excelsior award-winning school district.* Unpublished doctoral dissertation, State University of New York at Buffalo.

Sizer, T. R. (1991). No pain, no gain. *Educational Leadership, 48*(8), 32-34.

Spence, G. (1995). *How to argue and win every time.* New York: St. Martin's.

Sperry, R. (1973). Lateral specialization of cerebral functions in the surgically separated hemispheres. In F. J. McGuigan, & R. A. Schoonover (Eds.), *The psychophysiology of thinking* (pp. 209-222). New York: Academic Press.

Stacey, R. (1992). *Managing the unknowable: Strategic boundaries between order and chaos in organizations.* San Francisco: Jossey-Bass.

Tagushi, G. (1986). *Introduction to quality engineering.* Tokyo: Asian Productivity Organization.

Thompson, J. (1967). *Action in organizations.* New York: McGraw-Hill.

Tichy, N., & Ulrich, D. (1984). SMR forum: The leadership challenge—a call for the transformational leader. *Sloan Management Review, 26*(1), 59-68.

Trice, H. M., & Beyer, J. M. (1984). Studying organizational cultures through rites and ceremonials. *Academy of Management Review, 9*(4), 653-669.

Tushman, M., & Nadler, D. (1982). A model for diagnosing organization behavior. In M. Tushman & W. Moore (Eds.), *Innovation in organization* (pp. 153-168). Marshfield, MA: Pitman.

Vaill, P. B. (1978). Toward a behavioral description of high-performing systems. In M. W. McCall, Jr., & M. M. Lombardo (Eds.), *Leadership: Where else can we go?* (pp. 103-125). Durham, NC: Duke University Press.

Vaill, P. B. (1991). *Managing as a performing art: New ideas for a world of chaotic change.* San Francisco: Jossey-Bass.

Van Gennep, A. (1960). *The rites of passage* (M. B. Vizedom & G. L. Caffee, Trans.). Chicago: University of Chicago Press. (Original work published 1906).

Von Bertalanffy, L. (1975). *Perspectives on general system theory.* New York: Braziller.

Waldrop, M. (1992). *Complexity: The emerging science at the edge of order and chaos.* New York: Simon & Schuster.

Watzlawick, P., Weakland, J., & Fisch, R. (1974). *Change: Principles of problem formation and problem resolution.* New York: Norton.

Weber, M. (1947). *The theory of social and economic organization.* (T. Parsons, trans.). New York: Free Press.

Weick, K. (1977). Organization design: Organizations as self-designing systems. *Organizational Dynamics, 6*(2), 31-46.

Weick, K. (1979). *The social psychology of organizing.* New York: Random House.

Weisbord, M. (1987). *Productive workplaces.* San Francisco: Jossey-Bass.

Weiss, C. H. (1993). *Shared decision-making about what? A comparison of schools with and without teacher participation.* Cambridge, MA: Harvard University National Center for Educational Leadership.

Wheatley, M. (1992). *Leadership and the new science: Learning about organization from an orderly universe.* San Francisco: Berrett-Koehler.

White, P. A. (1992). Teacher empowerment under "ideal" school site autonomy. *Educational Evaluation and Policy Analysis, 14*(1), 69-82.

Wills, G. (1994). *Certain trumpets: The call of leaders.* New York: Simon & Schuster.

Withall, J., & Wood, F. (1979). Taking the threat out of classroom observation and feedback. *Journal of Teacher Education, 30*(1), 55-58.

Wohlstetter, P. (1995). Getting school-based management right: What works and what doesn't. *Phi Delta Kappan, 77*(1), 22-26.

Wood, F., Freeland, R., & Szabo, J. (1985). School improvement is more than school improvement. *Educational Leadership, 42*(6), 63-66.

Wood, F., & Neill, J. (1976). *A study of the effects of the | I | D | E | A | clinical workshop* (Report No. 2). Dayton, OH: Charles F. Kettering Foundation.

Wood, F., & Thompson, S. (1980). Guidelines for better staff development. *Educational Leadership, 37*(5), 374-378.

You, Y. (1993). What can we learn from chaos theory? An alternative approach to instructional systems design. *Educational Technology Research and Development, 41*(3), 17-32.

Zeleny, M. (1980). *Autopoiesis, dissipative structures and spontaneous social orders* (AAAS Selected Symposium 55). Boulder, CO: Westview.

CORWIN
PRESS

The Corwin Press logo—a raven striding across an open book—represents the happy union of courage and learning. We are a professional-level publisher of books and journals for K-12 educators, and we are committed to creating and providing resources that embody these qualities. Corwin's motto is "Success for All Learners."